UFOs

An up-to-date assessment of the current evidence for
Unidentified Flying Objects

Also in this series:

The Evidence for ALIEN ABDUCTIONS
   John Rimmer
The Evidence for BIGFOOT AND OTHER MAN-BEASTS
   Janet and Colin Bord
The Evidence for VISIONS OF THE VIRGIN MARY
   Kevin McClure

In preparation:

The Evidence for GHOSTS
   Andrew Green
The Evidence for PHANTOM HITCH-HIKERS
   Michael Goss

The Evidence for UFOs

HILARY EVANS

THE AQUARIAN PRESS
Wellingborough, Northamptonshire

First published 1983

British Library Cataloguing in Publication Data

Evans, Hilary
  The evidence for UFOs.
  1. Unidentified flying objects
  I. Title
  001.9'42   TL789

  ISBN 0-85030-350-8

*The Aquarian Press is part of the
Thorsons Publishing Group*

Printed and bound in Great Britain

CONTENTS

'THE EVIDENCE' Series is prepared by The Aquarian Press in collaboration with ASSAP (Association for the Scientific Study of Anomalous Phenomena) under the editorship of Hilary Evans. Each book in the series will give a comprehensive, impartial and up-to-date assessment of the evidence currently available for a particular phenomenon.

Each book is written by a recognized authority on the subject who is in a position both to give a comprehensive presentation of the facts and to analyse them in the light of his own experience and first-hand research.

————————— ● —————————

ASSAP (Association for the Scientific Study of Anomalous Phenomena) was founded in 1981 to bring together people working in different fields of anomaly research. It does not compete with other societies or organizations, but serves as a link organization enabling members of existing groups to share views and information and benefit from pooled resources. ASSAP issues its own publications, has its own research archives, library and other facilities, and holds periodic public conferences and training events in various parts of the country: ASSAP co-operates with local groups or, where none exists, may form one of its own.

ASSAP members include people from all walks of life who share a belief that it is the scientific approach which is most likely to solve these enigmas: they are neither uncritical 'believers' on the one hand, nor blinkered sceptics on the other, but are ready to go where the evidence leads them. If you sympathize with this attitude and would like to participate actively in our exciting pursuit of the truth, you may consider joining us. Write for fuller details to the Editor, Evidence Series, Aquarian Press, Denington Estate, Wellingborough NN8 2RQ.

ILLUSTRATIONS

Pictures of UFOs are of three sorts: photographs, witness sketches, and artists' impressions based on witness accounts. Photographs, discussed more fully in the text, are always suspect and generally spurious: it is, however, possible that a handful of them may be genuine. Witness sketches are very helpful in depicting what the witness thinks he saw, but are subject to faulty memory and inadequate drawing ability. Artists' impressions are always to be treated with reserve, but if they are prepared with the active co-operation of the witness, they may be helpful support to verbal testimony. So, though none of these illustrations can be taken as primary evidence, all convey information which can help us to judge the testimony.

Cover: UFO photographed over Hessdalen, Norway, by Arne Thomassen, 1982. This kind of ambiguous shape is far more typical than the structured 'spaceship' of popular belief – yet no less enigmatic.

Note: All illustrations have been supplied by the Mary Evans Picture Library. The author is grateful to those photographers and artists who have given permission for their work to be used. In cases where he has not been able to trace the copyright owner, he offers his apologies.

NOTE:
THE VALUE OF REPORTS

The evidence for UFOs consists of reports made by witnesses and checked by investigators. In principle, the witness describes what he observed, then the investigator evaluates his account in the light of the physical circumstances, the witness' character, the social context and other factors. Consequently, reports vary in value according not only to the integrity and observing skill of the witness but also to the reporting skill and integrity of the investigator.

Inevitably, a great many cases are worthless as scientific evidence, and a great many more must be regarded as dubious. Those cited in these pages were chosen because they seemed to be both honestly reported and competently investigated. But there are times when we must choose between citing an inadequately investigated case or ignoring it completely. Generally I have chosen to do the latter; but sometimes, to illustrate a point, I have had to do the former – for example, Case 31, the Vidal teleportation.

Whenever I am aware that the report is defective, I have indicated this. But my judgement is certainly not infallible. In the end it becomes a question of how far we are willing to trust witnesses and investigators whom we have never met. No sighting is ever reported with 100 per cent accuracy, no investigation is 100 per cent thorough: every piece of evidence cited here is to some degree unsatisfactory or imperfect. Such must always be the case in a field of study where the evidence derives from field observations rather than laboratory experiment.

The cases presented here are not of equal value, and some may be of no value at all. In Chapter Four I have attempted to assess how much we may rely on witness reports; but ultimately they are all, even when instruments are involved, subject to human interpretation. Any conclusion the reader comes to must be, like mine, provisional only, and dependent on the good faith of strangers.

ONE: THE UFO PHENOMENON

On 25 October 1955, the Office of Public Information of the Department of Defense, Washington, issued a news release which stated: 'The results of an investigation begun by the Air Force into the field of Unidentified Aerial Objects were released by the Air Force today. No evidence of the existence of the popularly-termed "flying saucers" was found.'

In 1964 NICAP – the National Investigations Committee on Aerial Phenomena – published a 184-page document presenting, densely packed in double columns, 746 cases selected from over 5000 signed reports which it claimed constituted evidence that UFOs exist.[73]

Somewhere between those two documents lies the truth, between official denials or disinterest on the one hand, and on the other a mounting mass of testimony by puzzled and often terrified witnesses of alleged extraordinary experiences. That testimony has been collected in a great number of journals, case reports and full-length books. There is a 750-page catalogue of 'encounter' cases in France alone,[55] and a list of 200 landing cases confined to Spain and Portugal.[7] There are catalogues of vehicle interference cases, of electro-magnetic effects, of UFO-related sounds and of the beings who are said to travel in them.[25, 113, 27, 161] And yet in 1968 the US Government spent $525,000 of its taxpayers' money on a 1465-page report, which concluded that the phenomena possessed no scientific interest.[37]

Alongside this paradox lies a second: this phenomenon which is of so little concern to science or to governments arouses in certain sections of the public a fervour which often reaches a mystical intensity. Of the hundreds of books and magazines devoted to UFOs, a large proportion are made up of sensational stories that are almost certainly not true, or no less sensational interpretations whose origins can be traced to a psychological or cultural response, where what the UFOs *are* is less important than what they *represent*. For some they are, quite literally, spaceships, bringing either cosmic saviours to rescue our planet, or sinister invaders with less kindly intentions. For others they have a religious significance – angelic or demonic as the case may be, engaged on missions of celestial import. For yet others, UFOs are inner visions projected outwards onto reality as expressions of some deep cultural need.

No phenomenon in history has lent itself to such a variety of interpretation, and at the same time generated such a diversity of response. At one extreme there are people who have given accounts of journeys made in UFOs to other worlds, of meetings with UFO occupants, of revelations transcending earthly knowledge and adventures surpassing human experience. If even a fraction of these accounts should be true, UFOs are one of the most extraordinary things ever to have happened on Earth. But there are also those who deny the very existence of UFOs altogether, and deny it with a vehemence that is itself remarkable, impelling an eminent astronomer, for example, to write three lengthy books demonstrating tht UFOs do not exist.[103, 104, 105]

In such a situation, the question 'Do UFOs exist?' cannot simply mean 'Are there flying objects which people are unable to identify?' – for of course there are. Rather, what we understand by the question is this: 'What evidence is there that, beneath all these reports, claims and beliefs, there exist objects which are neither mis-interpretations of things already known to exist, nor illusions of things that never did exist and never will, but something real and new to science?'

*   *   *   *

A great many people report seeing flying objects which they are unable to relate to anything they know. Often, other and more experienced people are able to tell them what they have seen – that it was something known but unfamiliar, such as a satellite or a meteor, or something familiar but seen in unusual circumstances, such as an advertising balloon festooned with lights or the planet Venus under exceptional meteorological conditions. And there are times when there just is not sufficient information for us to say precisely what was seen, but where it seems likely that, if we knew more, a natural explanation would be forthcoming.

Clearly, if all UFOs were potentially capable of being explained in terms of things we already know about, the problem would be relatively simple. It would be just a matter of matching the reported object against possible explanations, and seeing which fits best. But there are many cases in which either the appearance or the behaviour of the object is so totally different from anything we know, that we must say that either the witness is lying or mistaken, or he saw something outside our current knowledge.

Such cases have been reported sporadically throughout history, but their number has increased notably over the past thirty-five years. While much of the response has been emotional or partisan, there has been a persistent effort of objective investigation and analysis, steadily increasing in sophistication. The result of this effort is a quantity of data that makes the UFO one of the most thoroughly documented phenomena in history. We now have on record thousands of cases in which any explanation in terms of known objects is untenable. If those who saw them are telling the truth, they saw something unknown to human science. If they are lying or deluded, then a social phenomenon is taking place which is in itself unique in human history.

Can we believe these witnesses? Do their claims constitute evidence for the existence of a new phenomenon – not simply an *unidentified* flying object, but an *unknown* flying object? It is important to be clear what questions we are trying to answer, because there will be times in the course of our inquiry when we may be tempted to duck out of facing the implications of what we find. We are going to find that the UFO phenomenon is one of the most complex challenges, as it is one of the most puzzling, that man has ever had to confront. We shall find that much of the evidence is ambiguous, much contradictory, much seemingly irreconcilable with other evidence. Consequently, there will be a recurrent temptation to evade the challenge and opt for a simple reductionist explanation – that UFOs are 'simply' alien spaceships, or 'simply' hallucinations. Such explanations may perhaps be valid for some cases, but they are certainly not valid for all: they can be sustained only if we pick and choose among the evidence, discarding whatever does not suit our theory and selecting only what does.

But if our inquiry is to be scientific – and what value has it if it is not? – we must construct a hypothesis that accounts for the evidence *in its entirety*. The hypothesis may have to be immensely complex; to find it, we may have to call on several disciplines, consulting the psychologist as well as the engineer, the sociologist as well as the astronomer; and even then we may find that no single hypothesis will suffice. But whatever our answer, it must comprehend all the evidence, and all that the evidence implies.

A visual phenomenon

The UFO phenomenon is almost unique in one important respect: we have very little evidence except visual reports by people who claim to have seen it. If there were not so many of these reports, we could dismiss or ignore them as we do for rarer anomalies such as fairies or phantom ships, remarkable as the evidence is for both these phenomena. But UFO reports exist in tens of thousands, and even when we have weeded out those that are for one reason or another suspect, or for which we simply do not possess adequate data, we are still left with an astonishingly great number of people who have seen things which neither they nor anyone else are able to identify. The most evidential of these, with which we shall be chiefly concerned in our inquiry, are sightings by witnesses, seemingly sincere and honest, of objects which they describe as structured and designed, and which behave in a way that suggests that they are under some kind of intelligent control.

Even then, the task of interpreting them might be relatively simple were it not for some additional aspects:

* The objects seen, and the ways in which they behave, are almost infinitely diverse.

* The purpose and motivation of the craft are not only obscure, but often seem irrational by human standards.

* UFO phenomena are frequently accompanied by 'paranormal' manifestations, often similar to the 'poltergeist', and sometimes by apparitions of human-like figures.

* The mind of the individual witness is in some way related to his sighting: often there seem to be psychic dimensions to the incident – the witness has an intense emotional response, his character is altered for better or worse, he may claim further sightings and amazing adventures.

* Some physical evidence may be forthcoming, but while some of it is straightforward and supportive, such as the traces of an apparent landing, much is baffling and seemingly impossible, such as a frequently-reported ability to stop and re-start vehicle engines without causing damage.

* UFO sightings often have social aspects: they tend to be seen in 'waves', for example, and seem to favour certain locations, which are in consequence known as

'window areas'. We shall need to inquire whether these correlations are genuine, and if so how they relate to the central problem.

* UFO sightings closely parallel many incidents in folklore and even science fiction, in ways which seem to go beyond coincidence; we must inquire whether a similar cause could be operating in all such cases?

All this, and much more, is part and parcel of the UFO problem. Those who believe UFOs to be alien spaceships visiting our planet are understandably irritated by these complicating dimensions. But though in the end they may turn out to be irrelevant, or merely secondary, at this stage of our ignorance we cannot afford to neglect any aspect which might contain the vital clue. In the pages that follow I shall try to keep the subject as simple and matter-of-fact as possible: but we cannot deny the complexity of the phenomenon, and in considering even the most seemingly simple case we must be aware of its many possible parameters. Over and above *what* is seen, we must be aware of *where* and *when* it is seen, taking into account not only meteorological conditions but also such wider aspects as geophysical features. Above all, we shall want to know something about *who* saw the UFO – his physical, mental and emotional condition and his state of mind at the time, also his social and cultural background and his belief-system.

The nature of the UFO phenomenon

Why do so many factors need to be taken into account when asking a question as simple as 'Did so-and-so see such-and-such?' The answer will become apparent as we study representative cases; but let us start by taking a handful of relatively simple reports, picked almost at random from the files. Like most of the cases I shall be citing in this book, these are mostly not 'famous' cases, for I tend to agree with Belgian ufologist Jacques Scornaux when he writes, 'The refutability of a case is directly proportional to the publicity it receives'.[80]

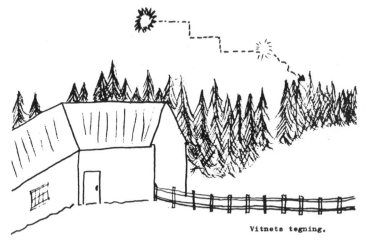

Sølen, Norway, 3.4.1980 (Case 1). Sketch by witness Fru Olsen.

Case 1   *Sølen i Engerdal, Norway*   *3.4.1980*

Fru Olsen was just going to bed when she saw, from a window on the upper floor of her home, in the heavily wooded Norwegian countryside, a very bright white light – so bright that she could not see any shape behind it. There was no sound. She watched its movements for about fifteen minutes as it moved slowly to the east, stopped, sank downwards a little, moved on again, stopped again, dropped again, then continued on its way till it seemed to drop slowly right into the forest. Because the terrain was flat and thickly covered with trees, it was not possible for her to judge distance or altitude, but she said the object looked about one-fifth the size of the moon.[125]

Case 2   *Bolazec, Bretagne, France*   *16.1.1966*

Eugene Coquil, a 23-year old carpenter, was driving along a country road at 4 am when he saw some lights out in a field accessible only by tractor. Thinking perhaps someone had had an accident, he stopped his car and started to

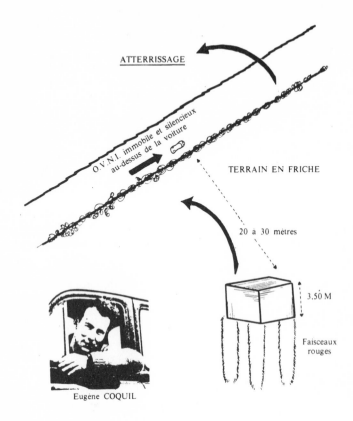

ATTERRISSAGE

O.V.N.I. immobile et silencieux au-dessus de la voiture

TERRAIN EN FRICHE

20 à 30 mètres

3.50 M

Faisceaux rouges

Eugène COQUIL

BOLAZEC 16 JANVIER 1966

Bolazec, France, 16.1.1966 (Case 2). Sketch by witness Eugene Coquil.

walk across the fields towards the light. He had gone only a few dozen metres when the object started to move silently towards him. The lights seemed too high above the ground to be a vehicle, and when it was about ten metres away, he saw that it was in fact airborne, four to five metres above the ground. At this point he ran back towards his car and got into it: the object followed him and hovered just a few metres above his car. He tried to get going but, perhaps due to panic, he had difficulty starting, though eventually he got away. He described the object as about the length of a car but wider, with four lights on the outside.[19]

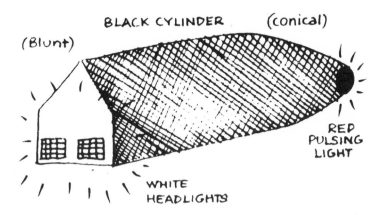

Partington, England, 14.11.1977 (Case 3). Sketch by witness.

Case 3   *Partington, Manchester, UK*   *14.11.1977*

About 5.45 pm one winter evening, four people got off a surburban bus bringing them out from the city centre: June, a 32-year old office worker, a female neighbour in her forties, and two men. They were acquainted only because they were frequent fellow travellers on the bus. They started to walk towards their various homes when all became aware of two unusual lights in the sky. They looked to be less than a kilometre distant across open fields, and about thirty metres above the ground: in all they occupied a segment of sky roughly equivalent to this book opened out and held at arm's length. The four witnesses were speculating about the lights when they were extinguished; this enabled them to make out that they related to a dark shape which started to move towards them. They stood in silence, and all later admitted to being frightened. All had an excellent view, and agreed in their description of a huge dark oblong with a pulsing

red light at one pointed end; they agreed, too, that it was
vast – 'like a huge floating restaurant' was one description.
After about two minutes it had passed over: one witness
hurried off in fright and informed the police, who took
the report seriously. It was suggested that there had been
other witnesses, but these were never traced.[56]

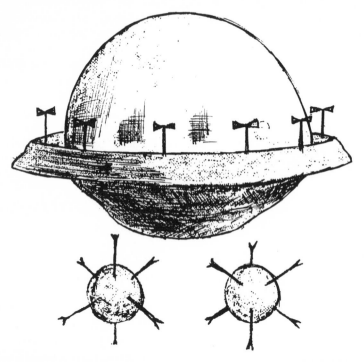

Livingston, Scotland, 9.11.1977 (Case 4). Artist's impression.

Case 4   *Livingston, Scotland*   *9.11.1979*

Robert Taylor, a 61-year old foreman forester, was
working in a forestry development area in full daylight at
about 10.15 am. He was on his way to inspect young
forest plantations when he rounded a corner in the forest
track and was confronted by a dome-shaped object, about
six metres wide, hovering silently just above the ground.

Almost immediately two smaller spherical objects – probably between 0.5 and 1 metre in diameter, and studded with spikes – rolled rapidly towards him. They attached themselves to his trouser-legs, one on each side, and began to tug him towards the larger object. He was overwhelmed by an acrid choking smell and lost consciousness. Some twenty minutes later he came round: the objects had disappeared, but there were substantial marks in the grass. At first he could neither speak nor walk; even when he recovered strength sufficiently to walk, it was only unsteadily. He dragged himself home where his wife gave the alarm: a doctor and the police were soon on the scene, while his work supervisor ordered the site of the incident to be fenced off. Despite press publicity, a thorough investigation was conducted by the police in co-operation with local UFO investigators. Taylor, who was well known in the neighbourhood, impressed everyone with his integrity, and nothing was found to contradict his story; for example, his clothing was torn in a way which was consistent with his account, while no alternative explanation made sense.[28]

Case 5   Cowichan, Vancouver Island, Canada   1.1.1970

Miss Doreen Kendall and Mrs Frieda Wilson were nurses at Cowichan District Hospital, working in the second-floor extended-care ward for elderly patients. At about 5 am Miss Kendall, attending a patient, went to the window to draw the curtains and let in some fresh air. About twenty metres distant, right above the children's ward on the third floor of the hospital wing to her left, she saw a big bright object clearly and in considerable detail: 'The object was circular and had what I guess you would call a top and bottom. The bottom was silvery, like metal, and was shaped like a bowl. There was a string of bright lights round it like a necklace. The top was a dome made of something like glass. It was lit up from inside and I could see right into it.' What she saw inside the dome was two male-like figures, facing to her right, away from the

Cowichan, Canada, 1.1.1970 (Case 5). Artist's impression by Brian James in *Canadian UFO Report*.

hospital. The one in front appeared taller, or perhaps was positioned higher, than the other. Their heads were encased in close-fitting dark material.

She was not at all frightened: 'I never felt so peaceful in all my life. I wish I could have talked to them.' The object began to tilt, enabling her to see more of the two figures. The one in front was standing in front of an instrument panel, which interested Doreen Kendall who had a special interest in racing cars and mechanics generally. 'The man in front was staring at the panel as if something very important was going on, and I wondered if they might have had mechanical trouble.' She saw the other figure turn and look at her. 'He seemed to look right at me but I couldn't see his face. I'm sure he saw me because then he touched the other man on the back. When the man in the back did this, the one in front reached down and took hold of something like a lever beside him. I'll never forget how deliberately he did it. He pushed back and forth and the saucer, or whatever you'd call it, started to circle slowly, still close to the building, in an anti-clockwise direction.'

She called Mrs Wilson over to the window. She confirmed the account though supplied less detail; she estimated the size of the object as fifteen metres in diameter, but saw neither the figures nor the ring of lights. Two other nurses, hearing the excited comments, rushed to the window, but saw only 'a bright light' receding in the distance; two other nurses saw nothing.

At about the same time, and in the same neighbourhood, a man and his wife returning from an all-night party saw a huge white light, as big as a house, hovering over their home. Though their description was of an oval or rectangular object, it may have been the same object seen from a different angle.[29]

Case 6   *Valensole, southern France*   *1.7.1965*

Maurice Masse, a 41-year old lavender grower, had gone to work in his field about 5.45 am. He was just enjoying a cigarette before starting his tractor, when he heard a whistling noise from the far side of a heap of rocks near which he was standing. Looking round the rocks he saw, about ninety metres away, a machine shaped like a rugby football, some three or four metres wide and 2.5 metres

Valensole, France, 1.7.1965 (Case 6). Artist's impression superimposed on photograph of alleged landing site.

high – the size of a smallish car. It was standing on six legs connected to a central pivot, and had a door and a transparent dome: M. Masse likened it to a monstrous spider. At first he thought it might be a helicopter, since they frequently landed on these fields: but he quickly realized this was no such thing. Then he saw two creatures bending down as though examining his plants: since his crop had recently been damaged by unknown vandals, he moved forward angrily.

He was about seven metres from them when one of the figures turned and pointed a pencil-like object at him, taken from a holder at its side: Masse found himself halted in his tracks, unable to move. The two figures stood watching him, but did not seem hostile; they seemed to be discussing him. They were about one metre tall, dressed in close-fitting grey-green clothing, with no headgear. Their heads were about three times the size of a human head, in proportion to their bodies: they had large ears, high cheeks, lidless eyes, no chins, and round holes for mouths.

The two beings returned to their machine; the door closed, the legs whirled and retracted, and the machine left the ground silently. When it was between fifteen and twenty metres away, it suddenly vanished. About fifteen minutes later feeling returned to Masse and he was able to move again: he worked until between 7.30 or 8 am, then went back to the village, where he told his adventure at a cafe. Being known and respected in the neighbourhood, his story was taken seriously and thoroughly investigated both by the police and by private UFO investigative groups: though some contradictions were noted, no reason was found to doubt his story, and some confirmation was obtained from other witnesses which seemed to support his claim. Physical traces were found on the site, which persisted and affected future crops until the field was ploughed over. Masse also suffered from psychological effects – he slept inordinately and experienced dreams of a psychic character.[56]

In selecting these examples, I have deliberately chosen relatively simple and unsensational cases, occurring to ordinary people in the casual course of their daily lives. None of these people was particularly interested in UFOs; they were not deliberately looking for them nor, so far as is known, were they subject to any other kind of delusion or preconception. In all six cases, the sighting came as a total surprise, to which the witness had to adjust while in the course of doing something quite trivial – going to bed, returning home, doing the daily work. In each case the witness responded with emotions ranging from mild puzzlement to complete bafflement; in each case subsequent investigation, while it has failed to discover the true explanation, has also failed to show that the witness in any way misreported the incident. In short, these things seem to have taken place as described, for all anyone can show to the contrary.

Of course, some of them are capable of some kind of explanation. For several of them, a helicopter might seem to offer an answer – behaving unusually for some reason, seeming silent by some trick of the wind, mis-reported as to speed, and so on. But though strictly *possible*, is it *probable* that not only all these, but the tens of thousands of similar cases, can all be due to misidentified helicopters hovering over hospitals in the early hours of the morning, buzzing motorists, paralysing farmers? Have vast numbers of people, many of whom see helicopters almost daily, suddenly become incapable of knowing one when they see one?

Clearly, witnesses can and do make mistakes. A high proportion of alleged sightings are explained by investigators who have the advantage of not being personally involved, and can supplement the common sense of the witness with their own experience and with access to informed sources such as airfields, observatories and meteorological offices. But if we respect such expertise when it finds an alternative explanation, we must also respect it when, as in our six examples, it fails to do so. In all such incidents there is, at the least, a serious case to be answered.

The investigation situation

As far as is publicly known, there is virtually no official investigation of UFOs anywhere in the world. For a while, when it was thought they might present a military threat, the United States armed forces made some effort to study the phenomenon. The security services, too, though this was officially denied at the time, also took a clandestine interest. When the phenomenon persisted without any indication of a threat to the nation's security, however, the government seemingly abandoned any formal study. Whether any covert investigation is being conducted remains a matter for speculation.

Other countries have shown even less interest, with the exceptions of Russia and France. The level of official involvement in Russia remains uncertain, but intermittent reports give evidence of spasmodic flurries of interest. France is the one country in the world where there has been any public recognition of the possible importance

of the UFO phenomenon: the gendarmerie have instructions to take UFO reports seriously, and a section of
the Centre National d'Études Spatiales (CNES), known as
the Groupe d'Étude des Phénomènes Aérospatiaux Non-
identifiés (GEPAN), enjoys a more or less official status,
though at the time of writing it seems that even this
initiative is aborting.

Consequent upon this widespread official lack of interest,
investigation of sightings and the study of the phenomenon
have been left to private groups and individuals who have
felt UFOs to be a matter of real concern. Some of these
have been spurred by personal, social and cultural
motivations which we shall need to examine; but an
impressive proportion have been open-minded investigators responding to the challenge of a baffling anomaly.

UFO investigation varies widely in effectiveness and
expertise. At one end of the scale are local 'UFO spotter
clubs' with a minimum of background knowledge and
little awareness of the broader context of the phenomenon:
for these, ufology is little more than science fiction come
true. But while such groups proliferated throughout the
early years, they are becoming rarer today. Instead a
progressively more serious and scientific approach is
being adopted, and this has resulted in a quantity of well-
investigated cases, matched by a substantial body of
research documents revealing a remarkable breadth of
outlook and profundity of analysis. Titles such as *UFOs
and the Limits of Science*, or *UFO Phenomena and the Behavioral
Scientist*,[141, 172] indicate the current direction of serious
ufology.

Complicating factors
The handful of cases cited above were selected for their
simplicity. What those witnesses saw was so clear-cut as
to defy explanation in terms of the familiar. Fru Olsen's
erratic light may have been a mistaken observation on her
part: yet what can it have been that made her think it so
remarkable?

Lights in the sky are of course the weakest kind of UFO

evidence because they afford so little information. As a rule ufologists have given up seeking to explain them beyond sorting out those which can be identified as aircraft, trains, cars, advertising planes, satellites, meteors and so on. The American investigator Harley Rutledge is one of the few serious researchers to have chosen deliberately to concentrate on lights in the sky.[131] As Professor of Physics at Southeast Missouri State University, he found himself being questioned concerning some

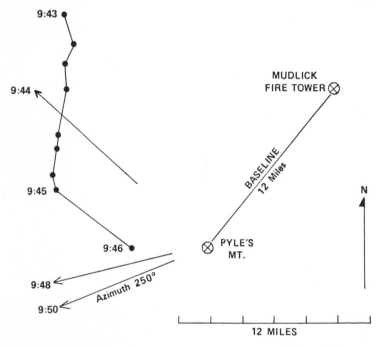

'Project Identification', Missouri, USA, 25.5.1973. The plan shows how an object was instrumentally monitored from two observation points separated by 18km. Synchronized observations enabled the object to be precisely located at 15 second intervals, establishing its course and speed from 9.43 to 9.46 pm. At that point the Fire Tower observation post lost track of the object which was thereafter observed only from Pyle's Mt. for a further two minutes, establishing direction but no precise distance. From Harley Rutledge, *Project Identification*.

anomalous lights that had been observed, over an extended period, in a hilly district some eighty kilometres from the university where he worked. As a scientist, he accepted the challenge: he collected a team of experts in various fields, put together an impressive array of instruments, and set off for the site with the expectation that two or three weekends of expert observation would suffice to find an explanation.

In the event it was not until seven years later that he published a report on his findings, based on nearly 2000 man-hours of observation. During that period 157 separate observations of 178 UFOs were instrumentally recorded, using a variety of procedures in which visual observation and photography were complemented by radar and other detectors, set up in separate locations for simultaneous observation. The great majority were simple lights in the sky like the one reported by Fru Olsen. There were no close encounters such as that of M. Masse: few instances offered any information as to shape and size. But all defied explanation in terms of any known natural or man-made phenomenon, and all indicated a degree of intelligent control and even awareness of the activities of the investigators.

So even if we choose to think that Fru Olsen may have mistaken a helicopter for a UFO, the fact is that others – experienced scientists – have established the existence of objects similar to the one she saw, but which were certainly *not* helicopters.

And if this is the case for the simplest of our six examples, how much more does it apply to the more complex. M. Coquil thought the lights he saw in the field came from a tractor; when he saw they were over the ground, he thought they must be from a helicopter. But the object that pursued him to his car did so in total silence: and one thing we know for sure about helicopters is that they are very, very noisy.

We may object that Coquil was alone, and that a man on his own – and even a young man of twenty-three in his own familiar neighbourhood – might at 4 am be panicked into thinking he saw something unusual, even into not noticing the sound of a helicopter. But in the Partington case it was not 4 am, it was 6 pm; and there were four independent witnesses to confirm that an enormous illuminated object had glided silently over their heads.

In the Livingston case we are back with the solitary witness, but now under daylight conditions where it seems hardly possible for an intelligent adult to have mistaken anything familiar for something so strange, causing him to lose consciousness and suffer such physical distress. All this apart from ground markings many centimetres deep, of a figuration incompatible with a tractor or any other piece of equipment which might have reached the site.

The hospital sighting had two witnesses, though admittedly only one saw the occupants. Even if Doreen Kendall imagined them, the object itself was undoubtedly seen by others: why should we suppose she is lying or hallucinating about the two figures? And what are we to say of the hundreds of other witnesses who claimed to have seen UFOs with occupants, often very similar to those described by Nurse Kendall: was it imagination at work in every instance?

Only a few, relatively speaking, have been fortunate enough to see, as M. Masse did, the occupants outside their vehicle. His story is the strangest of our sample, and is consequently the least believable. I suppose that most of us have a feeling that somehow his story is *not* true – that he is lying, or somehow mistaken. But only an outright lie, or a sincerely believed-in hallucination, can account for his case. In the full daylight of a summer morning, in an open and familiar field, a countryman, respected by his neighbours, is not going to mistake one thing for another, particularly not for a helicopter with which he is familiar.

And so it is with all our six cases. If the witnesses are dependable – and in none of these cases did investigators find any reason to doubt the witnesses – then either the incidents actually occurred or, which is almost equally improbable, something took place which made the witnesses *think* they actually occurred.

The question of IFOs

One of the questions begged by the term 'UFO' is: *unidentified by whom?* More often than not, though an inexperienced witness may see something he cannot identify, he can turn to someone more expert who will identify it for him. So it has been reckoned that some 90 per cent of reported cases enable the investigator to turn the UFO into an IFO – an *identified* object. Most sceptics would argue that all 100 per cent could be so explained if sufficient information were forthcoming. However, though 'insufficient data' may be a reason for rejecting many thousands of sightings as evidential, no ufologist would think of taking such cases as evidential anyway. The only cases of any value – the only kind of case we are interested in here in this book – are those where there *is* sufficient data to eliminate all known sources of mis-identification, natural or artificial.

If this were a UFO Investigator's Manual, we should need to devote considerable space to such possible alternative explanations. Many of them will indeed be mentioned in the course of this study, for we should always be aware, when considering any case, that there may be an explanation that would reduce a UFO to an IFO; but in every case cited as evidence in this book, such possibilities have been taken into account and discarded.

The wider context

Even if our six examples were isolated instances, they would be sufficiently remarkable: as representative of thousands equally valid, I suggest that they establish the fundamental fact of the UFO phenomenon. However, they were selected for their relative simplicity: to see the UFO phenomenon in its full complexity, we must note some additional features. First, we must recognize that UFOs are not entirely a phenomenon of our own time.

'Flying saucers' hit the world's headlines with Kenneth

Kenneth Arnold's sighting of 24.6.1947, as depicted – with flagrant disregard of the circumstances – on the cover of the first-ever issue of *Fate* magazine, which featured his article entitled 'I *did* see the Flying Saucers!'

Arnold's classic sighting of 1947, when he – an experienced pilot – saw a group of airborne objects flying at what seemed to be immense speed over a mountain range in Washington State, USA.[6] Controversy has simmered ever since as to what it was that Arnold saw: but whatever it was, for some reason his experience caught the world's imagination and UFOs, as a specific phenomenon, entered the public consciousness.

We shall be considering the social aspect of UFOs in the next chapter: here and now we should simply recognize that UFOs did not originate with the Arnold sighting, only the public awareness of them, which soon led to the notion that they might be piloted by extraterrestrial visitors. The sudden explosion of notoriety which began in the late 1940s was both a curse and a blessing. On the one hand, it saddled ufology with a burden of assumptions and connotations which have made dispassionate study very difficult; but on the other, by bringing the UFO into the public domain, it vastly increased the quantity of material available for study, forcing the world to take note of a phenomenon which had in fact been around for some time. Here are some examples of the sort of incident which form the 'pre-history' of the UFO:

Case 7   *Boston, Massachusetts, USA*   *3.1639*

James Everell, described as 'a sober, discreet man', was crossing Muddy River in a boat at about 10 pm, when suddenly a great light flared up in the sky above him and his companions. At first it hung stationary, seeming to be rectangular and about three metres across. Abruptly, the light moved swiftly across the Charles River towards Charlestown, then returned. Terrified, Everell and his companions cowered in their boat for some two or three hours while the light zigzagged across the river this way and that, in a way the witnesses compared to a pig trying to evade capture.[79]

Case 8   *Quincy, Illinois, USA*   *10.4.1897*

Many citizens saw an 'airship' in the night sky, describing it as a long slender cigar-shaped object between sixteen and thirty metres in length, seemingly metallic, with what appeared to be wings and some kind of superstructure. There were red and green lights along the hull, and a headlight like a searchlight in the nose. Some witnesses claimed to hear voices from it.[34]

This is just one case picked at random from a rash of sightings emanating from many parts of the United States in 1896-1897, most of which described aerial vehicles roughly similar to dirigibles. However, at this time there were no successful dirigibles in the United States, though there may have been some experimental models in the course of secret development: certainly there was no chance that any could have appeared in so many separate places and displayed such aeronautical proficiency. Other 'airship scares' were reported in England and New Zealand in 1909-1910 and elsewhere at other times.

Case 9   *Over Germany*   *1944*

Bill Leet, a United States Air Force bomber pilot, reported a ball of light which suddenly appeared alongside his plane 'like a light switch being turned on'. It seemed two-rather than three-dimensional, like the amber light at a traffic signal, but it did not resemble any earthly light. It stayed with the bomber for about forty-five minutes, then suddenly was gone. 'Our gunners wanted to shoot it down, but I ordered them not to. I told them if it was hostile, it would already have shot us down. Let's just try to figure out what it is, I told them.'[144]

Again, I have picked virtually at random one of the many reports of 'foo fighters', as they came to be called, which puzzled pilots on both sides towards the end of World War Two. Though seldom seeming to have any structure other than balls of light, they were at first presumed to be secret weapons until it was found that both sides were encountering them, both over France and later over the Pacific. The obvious temptation is to look for an explanation in terms of some such natural phenomenon as ball lightning, but no such phenomenon is known that is sustained for forty-five minutes, or at such an altitude. Additionally, for what it is worth, a majority of those who reported the foo fighters credited them with intelligent behaviour.

Case 10   *Sweden*   *8.1946*

An unnamed astronomer was studying clouds through a telescope when he saw a luminous point on the horizon. At first he thought it must be an aeroplane, then he realized it was travelling much too fast. Within ten seconds he could see that it was more like a projectile, torpedo-shaped, metallic in appearance and about thirty metres in length: though it was only two kilometres distant, there was no sound. Suddenly it exploded with a terrific light that momentarily blinded him, but there was no fire, sparks or smoke, though before the explosion it had been spewing blue and green smoke from its tail.[67]

While from the description this object sounds like the

Foo-fighter photographed over Germany (?) *circa* 1944. No details are available of this picture and it is possible that it relates to the Pacific combat area, where this type of aircraft is more probable.

rockets being used by the Germans towards the close of
World War Two, in fact it is just one of literally hundreds
of sightings of what came to be termed the 'ghost rockets'
which manifested over Scandinavia during the summer of
1946. Naturally it is tempting to look for an explanation
in terms of military weaponry; but apart from the fact
that it is hard to believe that any power would be so
irresponsible as to experiment with missiles over another
country's territory, if only for reasons of security, there is
the fact that no debris was recovered for certain, despite
the great many that traversed the country.

This brief selection shows not only that UFOs are not
necessarily a modern phenomenon, but also that it would
be a mistake to think of them as synonymous with 'flying
saucers'. They come in an almost infinite diversity of
shapes and forms. And as if that were not sufficiently
troublesome, there is the disconcerting fact that certain
forms seem to come into fashion then disappear again.
We shall be considering the implications of this later on,
for the clue to the UFO's nature is as likely to be found in
its paradoxical aspects as in straightforward observations.

A global phenomenon
Tens of thousands of alleged UFO sightings have been
reported, and many thousands of these have been investigated sufficiently thoroughly to establish that no easy
solution is forthcoming. Inevitably, distribution from
one part of the world to another is erratic: the number
reported from America and France, particularly, is out of
all proportion when related to geographical area or
population. However, this surely reflects the fact that in
both these countries there is an above-average reporting
machinery. Quite simply, a sighting occurring in France
is more likely to become known than one occurring in
Java or India, notwithstanding their density of population.
    So it is not surprising that the more developed the
country, the more UFO cases it has on file. But there are
differences between them that *are* surprising. For some

reason Germany and the Netherlands have played an insignificant part in ufology compared with, say, Spain and Belgium. This is surely a sociological fact, and a hint that the social aspects of ufology cannot be neglected.

The quality of reporting, too, varies from one region to another. We have a very great deal of material from Latin America, but that quantity alone would arouse suspicion even without the sensational character of so many of the reports. Thus, within the space of two months in 1982, a rash of amazing incidents was reported. In August a car-load of Venezuelans claimed to have been attacked by a great burning object which emitted red flames down onto the roadway. In the same month Argentinians blamed UFOs for raising a wind which caused a fire to spread; witnesses described 'a machine from hell' which fanned the fire like a flame-thrower. In the following month, Brazilians at Itacoatiara panicked because of a thing which came down from the sky, leaving people dizzy and women pregnant. Street barricades were erected, men took turns at trenches to repel invaders, families congregated in houses for protection. A farmer reported how his home was invaded by a many-coloured light; now he fears that his wife, who has already borne five children, may be impregnated again, this time by an extraterrestrial. At the same time, men who have been attacked by UFOs start speaking in treble pitch...[52] Clearly it would be rash to take seriously reports emanating from a populace capable of such reactions; but where do we draw the line as to what and who we are willing to believe?

Evading such uncertain decisions, other ufologists have tried to establish objective bases for research. Several valiant attempts have been made to compile comprehensive catalogues of UFO sightings, in the hope that they will reveal significant patterns. But such a catalogue is only worth as much as the material fed into it: so much depends on the standards of the original reporter. Any attempt at a scientific analysis on a global basis would need to be undertaken with the greatest diffidence.

Yet such a global overview is clearly desirable, and

must not be discouraged even though the theories formulated to date have been less than convincing. The best known is the 'orthoteny' hypothesis [107] proposed by some French ufologists, which sought to demonstrate that an above-average number of UFO sightings occurred along straight lines which were also related to other factors, even including the birthplaces of eminent people! Though some of the evidence for the pattern is persuasive, it seems preferable to regard it as an instance of the ability of random data to assume seemingly significant patterns.

A more recent variation on orthoteny has been 'isoscelie', the brainchild of a French ufologist named Fumoux[61] who came to believe that UFO sightings occur at the points of isosceles triangles in an above-chance proportion of instances. His findings were confirmed independently by computer, which is all the more remarkable since the data-base from which he was working was manifestly unreliable.[48] This did not prevent him arriving at some astonishing findings, including that UFO sightings during the 1954 wave were related to the Golden Number of 1.61803!

More methodical was the approach of New Zealand pilot Bruce Cathie, who in a series of books[31] has postulated a global grid system which from way back in history has criss-crossed the earth with a network of 'routes', and which is being exploited by interplanetary spaceships for navigational purposes and also as a source of motive power. This comes close to the geophysical hypotheses which we shall be considering in Chapter 7.

If any of these hypotheses could be shown to be valid, it would be an important step forward in marshalling the evidence, enabling us to discern some kind of meaning in what is otherwise a seemingly arbitrary collection of one-off cases. Unfortunately, even if they possess any partial validity, none of the global theories so far formulated promises to give us the whole answer.

The question of numbers is in itself a matter for almost infinite speculation. The French group 'GABRIEL' has calculated that if UFOs visited the earth uniformly, only 1 in 16 would even be capable of being seen by humans, because the rest would be over the sea or uninhabited regions. The time of day, coinciding with sleep or work, would reduce the figure to 1 in 64, and it is fair to say that at least half the UFOs will be dark silent shapes moving at night and so literally invisible. The fact that for two-thirds of the world no effective reporting agencies exist means that the figure is reduced to 1 in 384: additionally we could estimate that only 1 sighting in 10 is reported, and only one report in 10 is published. Consequently, the world at large only hears of 1 UFO in 38,400 that visits our planet![62]

Obviously, such a calculation is not intended to be taken seriously, since it contains too many unknowns. Nevertheless an independent survey by Ted Bloecher showed that even of those cases reported in local newspapers, only 1 in 20 is ever picked up by other interested parties and so made available for the purposes of research.[17]

Do UFOs visit our uninhabited deserts, our polar wastes, our uncharted jungles? We have no right to deny the possibility. Indeed, as this preliminary chapter has shown, we have little right to make any assumptions about what UFOs can or cannot do. Clearly we are confronted with a deal of evidence for one or more phenomena, which can reasonably be described as 'objects', which are seen either flying or in a situation that suggests that they are capable of flight, and which cannot be identified by reasonably experienced people. They are seen all over the world, by all kinds of people whom there is no reason to believe belong to any particular group or type; they are usually seen by these people in everyday circumstances, while going about their normal activities, and are often seen by more than one person at a time. They display no uniform appearance or behaviour pattern, and manifest no detectable purpose.

This is the phenomenon which we shall now approach from a variety of viewpoints in the hope that what is concealed from one viewpoint may be revealed to another.

TWO: UFOs AND SOCIETY

We do not have a UFO we can take to pieces, so far as is known (though there is some very tantalizing evidence to suggest otherwise). Instead, the UFO evidence consists chiefly of human testimony, which means that it is liable to all the distortions and biases that attach to all human testimony, whether for traffic accidents or murder. UFO witnesses, like any others, are creatures of their time and of their cultural environment. While there is no reason to doubt the sincerity of most witnesses, social factors inevitably affect the way in which they describe their adventures. Confronted by something they cannot explain, they naturally reach out for any way of making sense of what their eyes tell them they are seeing: inevitably they tend to do so in terms of their social background, their personal belief system. There is a natural desire to fit the unknown object into our 'consensus-reality', among the things we all accept as real.

But consensus-reality can take some very erratic forms. If angels or demons are real to you, you will not hesitate to accept them as viable explanations. If you are convinced that Earth is being visited by extraterrestrials, it will seem perfectly reasonable to you to explain an unidentified object as an alien spaceship.

Such has indeed been the most favoured UFO hypothesis, and we shall be considering it more fully in a later chapter. At this stage of our inquiry, we should simply note that commitment to a particular hypothesis affects a witness's belief system, and this will be liable to affect the way he makes his reports. Consequently it is essential for the investigator to be aware of such potential sources of distortion.

Saviours from the skies

Case 11   *near Clermont Ferrand, France*   *13.12.1973*

Claude Vorilhon, a successful racing driver, publisher of a motor racing magazine, married with two children, aged twenty-seven, was driving alone among the volcanic mountains of central France. Suddenly 'a kind of helicopter' descended through the fog: it was about seven metres in diameter, flat underneath and with a dome-shaped top, with a red light on the bottom and a very bright white light on the top. It came down to within two metres of the ground, where it hovered while a door in the bottom opened and a figure emerged. He was just over a metre tall, with long black hair and a beard, and wore a green one-piece suit. He halted about ten metres from Vorilhon, and started speaking to him in French; though, as he explained, he was from another planet, he spoke all languages of Earth. He told Vorilhon that his people had been observing him for a long time. Taking him inside the spaceship, he explained that Vorilhon had been chosen as an emissary who would tell the people of Earth of the visitors' benevolent mission. They had come to Earth to see what men were up to, and to watch over them. Over the next six days they dictated many messages and revealed many truths to Vorilhon, who was able to write a book based on their teachings and to create a sect, known as the Raelians.[156]

Vorilhon's book calls itself 'the book which tells the truth' and claims to contain 'the most important revelation in the history of mankind', which, if it is true, may well be a fair claim. But is it true? Evidently a great many people would like to think so, for when a lecture was announced by Vorilhon, to be given in a hall seating 150, 3000 people turned up.

If Vorilhon's story was unique, we might be more ready to give him the benefit of the doubt. Unfortunately, it is just one of many such revelations that have been published during the past few decades. They run to a pattern which has been repeated often enough to become a stereotype: an individual is alone, generally in an isolated location, when suddenly a spaceship arrives, spacepersons emerge, and he is told he has been chosen as some kind of go-between by the aliens, who are concerned to help us earthfolk through this particularly perilous phase of our history. Thus in 1954 London cab driver George King was told by a Cosmic Intelligence to prepare himself to become the Voice of Interplanetary Parliament, since when, as founder of the flourishing Aetherius Society, he has served as a link between his Cosmic Masters and ourselves.[89]

Case 12   Desert Center, California, USA   20.11.1952

George Adamski, a 61-year old man of Polish origin who had lived in the United States since the age of two, was an amateur astronomer who liked to style himself 'Professor', and the guru of a mystical-philosophical group named the Royal Order of Tibet. Just two months after Kenneth Arnold's famous sighting of June 1947, Adamski claimed to see 184 flying saucers over Mount Palomar, where he lived. In November 1952, acting on intuition, he made personal contact with Orthon, a Venusian, who confirmed that Adamski had been selected by them as their representative on Earth. Subsequently there were further meetings and interplanetary flights, described in a series of books.[95, 2] Though he died in 1965, Adamski continues to be a major cult figure with many loyal followers, despite the inconsistencies and untruths of his accounts. According to one of his closest adherents, he was a member of the Interplanetary Council, which he served so loyally that when he died he was granted a new body through which to work, and so is enabled to continue his vital role under another (unrevealed) identity.[158]

Apart from the manifest errors in his published accounts, and apart too from his questionable role as self-anointed guru, it is significant that Adamski's adventure closely matches a science fiction story published in 1946, Harold Sherman's *The Green Man*.[68] It tells how a professor of astronomy is driving home alone one night when his car unaccountably stops. He starts walking, and sees a large silver cigar-shaped object – like those Adamski later claimed to have photographed and travelled in – floating in the air behind some trees. An impressive figure emerges who asks the professor to be a special intermediary between mankind and an alien civilization, just as Orthon recruited Adamski. It may well be that Sherman's fiction provided the inspiration for all the subsequent contact stories, containing as it did so many elements which were later to become standard features.

Case 13   *Drakensberg, South Africa*   *27.12.1954*

Elizabeth Klarer was a 44-year old well-educated woman, whose interest in ufology was reflected by the reports she submitted to the highly respected American group NICAP. Subsequently she had her own UFO sightings, culminating in a meeting with Akon, an astrophysicist from Meton, one of the planets of Proxima Centauri. The relationship led to the birth of a son, who now lives with his father on Meton: Klarer, though she went to Meton to give birth to her child, had to return to Earth.[90]

Case 14   *Cergy-Pontoise, France*   *26.11.1979*

Three young men were loading an estate car in the early hours of a winter morning outside an apartment block on the outskirts of Paris, preparatory to working a street market, when they saw a UFO. One of them, Franck Fontaine, drove a little way to get a better look: when his companions rejoined the car, they found he had vanished. Precisely a week later he returned, unaware of having been away. Gradually he came to accept that he had been abducted on board a UFO and taken to an alien planet. In the course of the subsequent investigation, it emerged that the aliens were less interested in Franck than his companion Jean-Pierre Prévost, who had been selected as one of their emissaries on Earth. Though many inconsistencies were found in the account given by the young men, their cause was espoused by one of France's leading ufologists, Jimmy Guieu, who a very few months later wrote a book-length account of their adventure. The young men enjoyed a period of notoriety in which they made many public appearances and became cult figures with a considerable following.[71, 65]

Cergy-Pontoise, France, 26.11.1979 (Case 14). The chief witness, Franck Fontaine, emerges from the gendarmerie after reporting his safe return after being abducted by a UFO to an alien planet for a week.

Throughout history there have been people who have looked outside humanity for a saviour to deliver humanity from its sufferings: such is, of course, one basis of the world's religions.[35] It is reasonable, therefore, to see such cases as the foregoing as symptomatic of a search for a space-age equivalent for revealed religion. The millenarist character of the claims is emphasized by the 'messages' communicated by the Cosmic Saviours; typical of the vast mass of such literature are these extracts from the teachings of Ashtar, a high-ranking member of the Intergalactic Federation and the significantly-titled 'United Council of the Universal Brotherhood', with whom several contactees claim to be in touch:

The New World Order will come . . . it will be like nothing else that has ever taken place on your planet . . . Your planet will then be in a higher vibration. Your consciousness will be raised. George Washington and Abraham Lincoln were inspired by us. Jesus was one of us, he came as our messenger to the earth . . . There will be many changes within the next few years. Once the citizens of your country and the other countries around the earth band together, we will be able to land openly and speak with you. We would like to take you out of slavery, to have you join us here out among the stars.[10]

Inevitably the question arises, what truth if any is there in such claims? Did Vorilhon, Klarer or Adamski so much as see a UFO? The reader must make up his own mind; but in any case the total lack of confirmation, in all these instances, means that they have no evidential value. At the same time they are unquestionably of the greatest *sociological* value. The ufologist, intent on establishing the scientific facts, may resent the intrusion of such confusing material; but he must face the possibility that the same subconscious motivations that inspired these extreme cases may also be operating, less dramatically, in a great many more seemingly straightforward cases.

Agents of evil

While the majority of cult believers in UFOs see them as benevolent, a substantial minority take the contrary view. During the early years of the 'flying saucer' era there were many who saw them as a threat; books and films portrayed them as invaders, first from Russia or some other power, later from space. However, it became more and more difficult to sustain this view in the light of a complete absence of any sign of hostile intentions on the UFOs' part: even when they were reported in restricted air space over Washington, in 1965 for example, they did not seize the opportunity to zap the White House, as an invading force might have been expected to do.

There is, however, another school of thought that sees the UFOs as more sinister than any flesh-and-blood invader from another planet; which sees them as the instruments of spiritual powers, good and evil, who are warring for the souls of mankind in a cosmic conflict whose battleground is the universe itself. 'The basic purpose behind all UFO phenomena today', according to physicist and astronomer Arthur Eedle, 'is to prepare for the coming of Antichrist, and the setting up of World domination under the Devil.'[45] Similar views have been expressed by a surprisingly large number of writers.

Case 15   Charleston, South Carolina, USA   18.3.1978

Thirty-year old truck driver Bill Herrmann was watching a metal disc-shaped object, apparently about twenty metres in diameter, in the sky near his home. Suddenly it dropped down in front of him; he fell backward, felt himself surrounded by light and tugged upward, and lost consciousness. Later he came to in an open field, miles away. Subsequently, thanks to hypnosis, he was able to recall being on board the spacecraft, where he was examined by foetus-like aliens about 1.5 metres tall. He had no question that his experience was 'a Satanic delusion'. Since then he has had several more such encounters, but renounces them in the name of God. Herrmann is a fundamentalist Baptist.[139]

The demonic cultists are telling substantially the same story as the believers in cosmic saviours, but assigning the UFOs to the villain rather than to the hero. A further school of thought supposes both sides to be similarly equipped:

Case 16   *Highbridge, New Jersey, USA*   *1956*

Howard Menger, a self-employed sign painter, met a group of space people who informed him that he and his second wife were in fact Venusians. They told him that 'this earth is the battlefield of Armageddon, and the battle is for men's minds and souls'. While the beings Menger encountered were, luckily for him, 'goodies', opposing them was an anti-God group who are exploiting certain key figures in the governments of the world. The gathering swarms of UFOs are a sign that the time of crisis is approaching. [102]

For those who do not share such a belief system, it is hard to take seriously an interpretation of UFOs as either angelic or demonic chariots. But while most theorists along these lines tend to be strong on dogmatic assertion, weak on factual support, a few (notably Wilson and Weldon[159]) have made out a documented and well-argued case. Most ufologists would ascribe this approach to the cultural history and social background of those who adopt it, but that does not lessen the importance of recognizing and studying their viewpoint. Such beliefs can not only distort the way a witness reports his experience, but also determine what he believed he saw in the first place.

Abductions

One of the aspects of ufology which encourages scepticism is the way different types of UFO experience seem to occur in waves as though one kind of incident came into fashion as another went out. Today, naive contactees like Adamski, who proliferated in the 1950s, are relatively rare; instead there is a growing number of cases usually labelled 'abductions', of which this was the archetype:

Case 17   *Indian Head, New Hampshire, USA*   *19.9.1961*

Barney and Betty Hill were driving at night in a sparsely populated district of New England when they saw a strange object which they decided must be a UFO. It followed them for about fifty kilometres, then came down low and hovered close by the road. The Hills stopped to look at it: Barney got out of the car and approached the object, claiming to see occupants. They then continued their journey, but suffered psychological troubles which they connected with their experience. Betty had dreams in which they were taken aboard the UFO and subjected to a medical examination; Barney suffered from depression and exhaustion, which eventually led to their seeking psychiatric help. Hypnosis was prescribed, and while hypnotized, both witnesses confirmed that Betty's dreams were in fact a true account of experiences, which they had been conditioned to repress by their abductors. According to this account, after driving on they unaccountably took a side road, where they were halted by a group of aliens who took them into their vessel and subjected them, independently, to a medical examination. The vividness of the remembered experience, the way in which Barney's narrative dovetailed with Betty's, encouraged the witnesses themselves, and many commentators, to believe that they really underwent the experience they described, though their doctor remained sceptical, inclining to the probability that they had experienced some kind of shared fantasy.[59, 47]

Since 1961 there have been a good many such cases; often these have involved witnesses of a high calibre, such as police officer Herb Schirmer, who in December 1967 underwent a very similar experience in the course of a

Indian Head, USA, 19.9.1961 (Case 17). Drawing by Barney Hill of the spaceship and its occupants.

patrol.[18] For the ufologist, such accounts are more acceptable than the 'space-brother' type of contact case: the events tend to be logical, there is often a link with a possibly genuine UFO sighting, and there is a refreshing absence of cult-type message. On the other hand, the tendency for such cases to occur to isolated persons in remote locations, with no means of confirming their temporary absence from the earthly scene, does not encourage belief.

When the first such cases occurred, the fact that witnesses recalled their experiences so vividly under hypnosis was taken as strong support. But we have learnt so much about hypnosis during the last few years, that we must recognize the possibility of alternative, if often very complex, psychological processes. Abduction cases are so remarkable, and promise so much insight into psychological processes, that they merit study as a phenomenon in their own right, and are the subject of a subsequent volume in this series.[129] The reader must make up his own mind what, if anything, they contribute to the sum of UFO evidence: but as with the demonic and angelic interpretations, they indicate, at the very least, cultural factors of which the ufologist must be aware.

UFOs and the individual

One reason why abduction cases are more acceptable than contact cases is because the witness usually makes no claim to have been selected: the implication is that it might have happened to anybody, that Schirmer or the Hill couple just happened to be the first to come along.

Paradoxically, however, there are indications in many cases that there exists some kind of psychic link between the witness and the UFO or its occupants. While such a claim is anathema to down-to-earth ufologists, the psychological dimension can no more be disregarded than the sociological dimension we have noted earlier in this chapter. There are many cases in which the psychic or parapsychological link is central to the events and an essential element of the evidence.

Case 18   *South-east France*   *2.11.1968*

A doctor is wakened at about 4 am by his young son, who points from his cot to the window. The witness looks out and sees flashes of light above the valley facing him: a storm is evidently on its way. Then he sees two disc-shaped objects, each emitting a downwards beam of light; they move in his direction and fuse into one object, which continues to move towards him. Suddenly a beam of light is projected at him, and the UFO explodes into a cloudy shape which disperses. The entire episode has taken about ten minutes. Shaken, he writes an account of the happening, and wakes his wife to tell her of it. Suddenly he realizes that a pain in his leg, the result of an old war wound, has vanished, along with the swelling from the injury. He goes back to sleep, but talks in his sleep: his wife notes the phrase 'Contact will be re-established by falling down the stairs on November 2nd'.

The next day he sleeps through until the afternoon; when he wakes he remembers nothing of the previous night's adventure, not even when his wife shows him his notes. Later that afternoon he has a fall on the stairs, and they are reminded that the date is November 2nd; with the fall, memory of the event comes back. Though his leg injury continues cured, he has a pain in his umbilical region; a strange triangular mark appears for which doctors have no explanation. More curiously still, a similar mark appears on his young son.[56]

It is tempting to reject so bizarre a case out of hand; but it has the impressive support of Aimé Michel, France's most respected ufologist, who was personally acquainted with 'Dr X' and studied the case in depth. But if we accept the case as evidential, we have also to accept some kind of mental psychic link, suggesting a rapport between the witness and the objects or whoever controls them. At the same time, the fact that it was his young son who first drew his attention to the objects seems to establish some degree of physical reality.

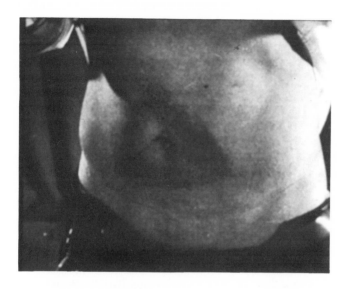

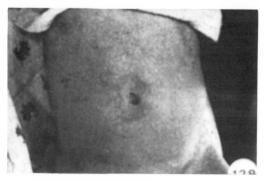

South-east France, 2.11.1968 (Case 18). Photographs showing the unexplained marks which appeared round the navels of both 'Dr X' and his fourteen-month-old son after their sighting.

Such 'psychic connections' take many forms. In 1981 UFO investigators in Bristol studied a housewife who was intuitively aware of the presence of UFOs, and, when they manifested, could mentally direct their movements in the presence of observers. Rutledge, in America,[13] has had similar experiences, and there are several witnesses, such as Luis Jose Grifol in Spain, who have produced photographs by the dozen which they allege to be of UFOs with whom they are somehow in communication.[66]

Case 19   South Ashburnham, Massachusetts, USA   25.1.1961

The case of Betty Andreasson, which has been studied in depth by competent ufologists, brings together several of the themes noted in this chapter. Betty, a housewife, was at home with her seven children, her father and her mother; her husband was in hospital following a car accident. About 6.35 pm the lights went out, and through the kitchen window a pulsing orange-red light could be seen outside the house. Betty's father saw a group of small creatures approaching: a moment later five humanoids entered the kitchen. While the rest of the household were placed in a state of suspended animation, the leader of the visitors communicated with Betty telepathically. The beings were about 1.5 metres tall, with large heads and wraparound eyes.

Betty was taken out to a small UFO, some six metres in diameter, which was resting on the side of the hill that sloped down to her backyard: it was of the classic shape – like a plate inverted on another, with a dome on top. She was taken up in this UFO to a larger ship where a physical examination took place, then on to an alien place, seemingly underground, where she underwent a painful and traumatic religious experience, which seemed directed at her as an individual rather than an all-purpose display which any witness might have experienced.

She was returned home at about 10.40 pm, to find her family still in a state of suspended animation. All went to bed: they seemed to have only a vague awareness of the events. Betty herself was so ignorant of UFOs that she regarded her experience as more religious in character, she being a devout Christian.[58]

The Andreasson affair is extremely complex, and rich in

overtones both psychological and cultural. The witness was strongly affected in outlook and temperament by her experience: this is true of a great many witnesses who claim to have had such intimate experiences. In 1980 Dr Leo Sprinkle, of the University of Wyoming, held a three-day conference at which a number of alleged contactees told their histories and compared their responses: the resemblance to the experience of religious conversion, of being 'born again', was notable in many cases.[130]

It may well be that all the cases cited in this chapter merit study by the psychologist or the sociologist, or even by the psychical researcher, rather than the ufologist. Nevertheless, insofar as a UFO connection is alleged by the witness, it would be premature to dismiss them as irrelevant to our inquiry. There are three possible scenarios:

* These cases are as factual as any others produced as evidence for the existence of UFOs.

* They commence as factual cases, but the physical event triggers a subjective response in the mind of the witness, who fantasises the rest in terms suggested by his psychological and/or socio-cultural situation.

* They are fantasy from beginning to end, based on no factual event but on the witness's unconscious awareness of such cases, which his imagination utilizes because they provide an appropriate form of expression.

Such cases may be too ambiguous to use in assessing the evidence for UFOs, but they force us to recognize that the UFO witness is very far from being a dispassionate observer. Both as an individual, with his own psychological make-up, and as a member of society, with its own beliefs and values, he is motivated and prejudiced as to what he thinks he sees and how he reports it. All evidence for UFOs is suspect until these psychological and social dimensions have been taken into account.

THREE:
THE PHYSICAL EVIDENCE

Almost from the day that 'flying saucers' first impinged on the world's attention there have been rumours that one or more have crashed, and that governments are keeping and studying them in the utmost secrecy. Some accounts even include the UFO occupants, dead or alive. Though there is no certain proof that these stories have any foundation in fact, it must be confessed that there is a good deal of impressive circumstantial evidence. It is at least clear that some governments, particularly that of the United States, are concealing *something*.[13, 47]

The discovery of a crashed UFO would be second only to the classic 'landing on the White House lawn', of which all ufologists dream. We should then know for certain that UFOs are physical artefacts, and would have a starting point for building up complete information about their nature, origin, purpose, mode of propulsion and other puzzling aspects.

UFO fragments
The next best thing to a whole UFO is a piece of one. A number of fragments, allegedly from UFOs, have been reported over the years.

Case 20   Near Les Ecureuils, Quebec, Canada   12.6.1960

Following a 'sonic boom', which shook the whole neighbourhood, a beachcomber found several fragments of metal, of which the largest was more than two metres in length and weighed more than 1200 kilograms, on the shore of the St Lawrence River. Examination provided indications that it consisted of fused metal, containing various artefacts such as fabricated pipes and some kind of electronic component. Several attempts at analysis produced conflicting results but no conclusion. While there is no clearer tie-in with UFOs than the sonic boom, neither does any explanation in terms of man-made objects make sense.[140]

A similar ambiguity applies to other instances of fragments, of which perhaps a half-dozen have been reported with any degree of credibility. The best known is the 1957 case at Ubatuba, Brazil, in which some pieces of metal were collected by witnesses who had seen a UFO disc explode over a beach. Unfortunately, the people who sent the fragments in a letter wrote so illegibly that they could not be traced, nor could investigators track down a single eye-witness to the alleged explosion. Analysis of the metal revealed it to be a rare sample of magnesium, but not so rare that an extraterrestrial source is conclusively indicated.[140]

Another frustrating case is that of a Mr Richardson, driving with a friend on 13 July 1967, who came round a corner of a country road to find his way blocked by a large luminous object which he could not brake in time to avoid hitting before it vanished. There was little damage but he informed the police, who accompanied him back to the scene of the accident. There was nothing to see on site except Richardson's skid marks; but the next day he went back there on his own and found a fragment of metallic material which he sent to the investigative organization APRO. Though he told nobody else, so he claimed, and though APRO told nobody except one of their investigators, Richardson received a visit from menacing callers who threatened 'If you want your wife to stay as pretty as she is, then you'd better get the metal back.' If the facts are as stated, then someone, possibly government agents as they claimed, not only believed Richardson's story but believed the fragment to be important: but nothing more was heard from the threateners, and the fate of the fragment is likewise unknown.[5]

Even when fragments have been subjected to expert analysis, the results have always been ambiguous. Moreover, not one of the findings has been associated with a convincing UFO sighting. Consequently, fragment cases do not provide us with any evidence of real value.

Another physical substance associated with UFOs is a gossamer-like material popularly known as 'angel's hair', which has often been observed falling or having fallen from the sky in large masses, sometimes in association with UFO sightings. Of many cases, this is probably the most clear-cut indication of a UFO connection:

Case 21   *Oloron, France*   *17.10.1952*

M. Prigent, while at home at 12.50 pm with his wife and children for the midday meal, from the school where he was headmaster, saw a fleecy cloud of unusual shape, and above it a long narrow cylindrical object. It was white

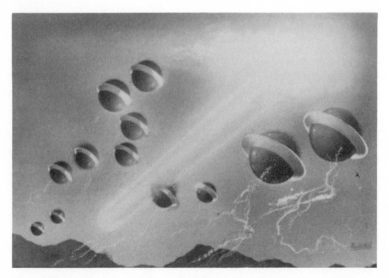

Oloron, France, 17.10.1952 (Case 21). Artist's impression.

rather than luminous in colour, had a distinct shape, tilted at an angle of 45 degrees, and was emitting puffs of white smoke from the top: he estimated its altitude as between 2000 and 3000 metres. Ahead of it were travelling about thirty smaller objects; to the naked eye they seemed shapeless, like balls of smoke, but through binoculars it could be seen that they were red spheres with a yellow ring round, like the planet Saturn. All were travelling in a zigzag path, the small objects moving in pairs. When two objects moved away from each other, they seemed to leave a whitish trail like an electric arc. In addition they left long trails of a substance which disintegrated and drifted to the ground. For hours afterwards, trees, telephone wires and roofs were festooned with the stuff, which, as numerous witnesses testified, became gelatinous, sublimated, and finally vanished completely. Experts tried in vain to discover its nature.[106]

'Angel's hair' is frequently attributed to drifting spiders' webs, and there seems little doubt that in some cases this is the correct explanation. But unless M. Prigent and his family were imagining their sighting, it would certainly seem in this case at least that something more exotic than spiders' webs was involved.

Traces

If the fragments alleged to have fallen from UFOs are ambiguous, hardly less so are the traces they are said to have left. There is a regrettable tendency among the more gullible UFO investigators to attribute any inexplicable mark on the ground to a visiting UFO, but the connection is not always as clear-cut as at Livingston (Case 4) or Valensole (Case 6).

Traces allegedly left by UFOs chiefly consist of the marks they leave behind after landing or standing on the ground. Swirling circular patches in vegetation, especially in standing crops, are frequently reported: Australia in particular has produced a number of cases of 'nests' where a UFO connection seems indicated. However, unusual meteorological effects are undoubtedly the cause of some, and perhaps of all, such cases.[122]

In 1980 American researcher Ted Phillips reported that he had on file 1058 cases of landing traces and residue. Of these, probably the most convincing are those in which imprints in the soil, often indicative of very great weights or pressures, are found in patterns which could correspond to the landing gear of a UFO. At Valensole (Case 6) investigators found that where the witness claimed the UFO had stood, there was a cylinder-shaped hole 18 centimetres in diameter and forty centimetres in depth, apparently caused by the central shaft described by M. Masse – a very unusual configuration, for most UFO witnesses describe a set of splayed 'legs' when indicating landing gear. Indeed, four smaller imprints were found surrounding the central hole at Valensole. Soil analysis of the hole showed that it contained 18 per cent calcium, whereas in a control sample the proportion was negligible. The traces were visible for more than four years afterwards, disappearing only when the ground was ploughed up.

Clearly, traces are of evidential value only when they are indisputably associated with a UFO sighting; from which it follows that evidence afforded by traces is only as good as that for the sighting with which they are associated. In such cases, the traces could indeed provide confirmation; in the Livingston case (Case 4) it is hard to believe that Taylor either would or even could have made the traces himself. Often, moreover, the indication that a force of many thousands of kilograms would be needed to make the imprint is sufficient to rule out all but a most sophisticated explanation. It seems reasonable to conclude, therefore, that though as primary evidence traces are too ambiguous, as back-up confirmation they can be of considerable importance.

Effects on people
Many of those who come into contact with UFOs, or even come close to them, report physical effects.

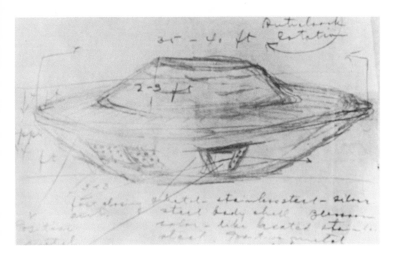

Falcon Lake, Canàda, 20.5.1967 (Case 22). Witness sketch.

Case 22   *Falcon Lake, Canada*   *20.5.1967*

Steven Michalak, age fifty-one, was prospecting alone in wooded, rocky terrain when he saw two oval UFOs, glowing red, descending rapidly to the ground. One of them landed about fifty metres from him: the other hovered for a while, then moved away at great speed. He observed the landed object for about thirty minutes, during which time it changed colour from red to grey to a 'glowing steel' hue. A door opened through which came a purple light, and warm air with a sulphury smell. Michalak approached closer: at about twenty metres distance he heard voices from inside the object. He tried calling to the occupants but obtained no response, so he went closer still and put his head inside the opening, taking the precaution of putting lenses over the goggles he carried for protection while prospecting. Inside the object he could see a maze of lights with beams running in every direction, seemingly at random. He was inspecting the surface of the object when it tilted and he felt a scorching pain in his chest. As he touched the machine his rubber-coated glove melted and his shirt caught fire. He tore the shirt off: at the same moment the object lifted off the ground and shot rapidly away, quickly vanishing.

Afterwards, Michalak felt ill as well as frightened, and on examining his chest he found he had marks forming a kind of grid-pattern, corresponding to burns on his shirt. Subsequently he developed rashes. On returning to the site with investigators – which necessitated several trips as he found it hard to remember the location – an outline of the UFO's shape was discernible on the ground, and trees nearby were withered or dead.[21]

Case 23   *Near Huffman, Texas, USA*   *29.12.1980*

Betty Cash, age fifty-one, together with friend and work colleague Vickie Landrum, age fifty-seven, and Vickie's seven-year old grandson Colby, were motoring along a country road at about 9 pm when they saw a luminous, fiery looking object about five kilometres ahead of them. They watched it descend to treetop level, and heard a beeping sound. As they drew closer they could see that it was considerably larger than a car, and was now so low that if it had not been over the roadway, it would surely have burned the trees. At a distance of about sixty metres Betty, afraid to drive beneath the object, stopped the car, and all three got out to watch it. Even at this distance they could feel the heat; after two or three minutes the boy grew scared and got back into the car, and his grandmother got in too to comfort him though, being a devout Christian, she connected the object with Jesus Christ. Betty continued to stay out for a while longer: she noticed that the car exterior had become extremely hot.

Eventually the object moved away, and the witnesses saw that it seemed to be escorted by a number of helicopters which they later identified as being of the CH47 and other types used by the US armed forces, though government officials denied that any of their aircraft were operating in the area.

Betty Cash arrived home at 9.50 am feeling distinctly

ill; she had a swollen neck, earlobes and eyelids, and blisters on her face: her eyes were almost closed so that she was unable to see properly for several days, and she suffered serious hair loss. For some time she was unable to eat, and was subject to vomiting and diarrhoea: she spent fifteen days in hospital, and even after returning home was tired, subject to headaches and unable to work. This persisted for more than a year. The two other witnesses were less seriously affected, presumably because they had got back into the car sooner: but they suffered the same symptoms to a lesser degree and the boy was troubled with nightmares.

Another witness confirmed the UFO sighting and three more saw the helicopters. Despite official denials, there seems a strong probability that what the witnesses saw was some kind of secret government project: but investigation, which is still proceeding, has yet to reach a firm conclusion.[148]

Near Huffmann, Texas, 29.12.1980 (Case 23). Artist's sketch by Kathy Schuessler, wife of principal investigator, for MUFON *Journal*, November 1981.

This type of case provides the strongest evidence to date for UFO effects. The medical evidence is incontrovertible, and it is fortunate that the case was being competently investigated within days of its occurrence. While there is a strong case for suspecting government involvement, it is hard to imagine that a secret project would be tested in so public a place, and the alternative suggestion has been made that perhaps the American government was assisting an extraterrestrial vessel in trouble!

However, even if it should be demonstrated that the case was one of a maverick American project, the same can hardly be said of the dozens of other instances in which UFO witnesses have suffered physical consequences following their sighting. Headaches, nausea, diarrhoea and vomiting are frequently mentioned by witnesses who have not necessarily been close to the object; sometimes this can be associated with a light beam directed at the witness, but not in every case, nor are such symptoms encountered in every case. Yet again, the evidence is ambiguous.

Radar cases

Just as astronomers have learnt of the existence of celestial bodies, invisible even to instruments, by the effect they have on visible bodies, so – in the absence of tangible evidence for UFOs – it is theoretically possible to infer their existence from their effects.

Radar is an obvious example. Radar scanning is being carried on throughout the world all the time, sweeping large areas of the sky both from the ground and from the air. UFOs may be picked up in the course of normal operation, or, if reported and located, may be watched for on the radar screens.

As long ago as 1964, the American organization NICAP was able to list eighty-one cases indicative of radar detection of UFOs occurring between 1948 and 1962. Fifty-nine of these combined radar and visual sightings, eleven combined radar detection from both ground and air, and one was photographed as well. This case is typical:

Case 24   *Yaak, Montana, USA*   *Summer 1953*

Sergeant William Kelly and his colleagues picked up six unidentified targets on their screens. In five sweeps of the antenna (taking about one minute) the targets changed direction five times, sometimes making ninety-degree turns. When the radar indicated that the objects were within sixteen kilometres of the station, the crew went outside to see if they could see anything. They saw six objects in trail formation, but which switched to other formations. Their speed was calculated as between 2200-2500 km/h; at that time the world air speed record was just over 1200 km/h. Other radar stations were notified, and they too tracked the objects.[113]

Radar evidence is particularly vulnerable to sceptical criticism, because it is notorious that radar picks up all kinds of anomalous signals, being unable to distinguish between many types of target. Often, it can only indicate that 'something' is there, which may be an aircraft but may also be a flight of birds, a balloon, or a natural phenomenon such as a layer of air of a different temperature.

Clearly, though, radar operators come to be familiar with such anomalies, for if they did not, the system would be next to useless. Consequently, when a radar operator says he has picked up something he cannot explain his statement cannot be simply dismissed. Even if we judge only by the number of puzzling cases that have been published, they seem too frequent to be attributed to chance or coincidence; but we must bear in mind that radar systems are mostly operated either by government services, or by such quasi-official organizations as airport authorities, operating under strict security. So it may reasonably be assumed that the number of anomalous radar cases the public gets to hear about is only a minute fraction of those that actually occur.

Nonetheless, because radar is liable to pick up false targets, no radar-only case can be considered of high evidential value, even when reported by experienced operators under ideal conditions. When, however, that report is coupled with a visual sighting, as in Case 24, the evidence becomes extremely strong, for it shows that whatever the eye-witnesses saw was something capable of giving a radar return.

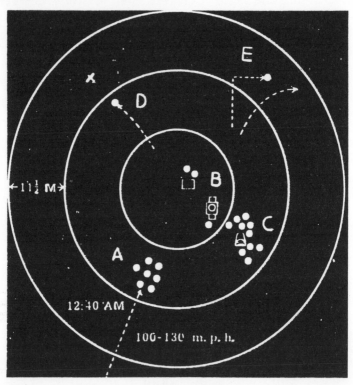

Washington, D.C., USA, 20.7.1952. Diagram depicting UFO activity between 11.40 pm-3 am reported by radar operators but with dubious visual confirmation.

A – seven objects approach Washington from the South
B – several objects over central Washington
C – several objects over Andrews Air Force Base
D – object tracks airliner
E – object makes sharp right-angle turn

Source and authenticity unknown.

Case 25   *Torino, Italy*   *30.11.1973*

Riccardo Marano was about to land his private Piper Navajo at Caselle Airport, at about 7 pm, when the control tower warned him of an unidentified object 400 metres over the runway. Marano flew towards it but it moved away, flying in an irregular fashion, manoeuvring as no plane could in horizontal and vertical leaps. Seeing it cover nearly 4800 metres – vertically – in two seconds, he estimated its overall speed at about 5000 km/h. The commandant of the airfield saw the object on radar, which indicated a size comparable to a DC8: later it was detected by military radar. The visual sighting was confirmed by two professional pilots from Alitalia, as well as by several civilian witnesses.[20]

French ufologist Michel Monnerie has noted discrepancies in the reports of this case and concludes that the radar operator picked up an echo (perhaps of a weather balloon), went to look out for a visual sighting, saw the planet Venus, which he failed to recognize, and indicated it to Marano as being over the runway. The rest he ascribes to collective suggestion – Marano, advised of a strange light, duly saw one, imagining the abrupt movements, the high speeds and so on; likewise for the other witnesses.[110, 111] The reader will have to decide whether Monnerie's explanation is more credible than the incidents as reported.

It is undeniable that radar is peculiarly subject to misinterpretation; but as with other physical effects we have noted in this chapter, it can give important confirmation of the visual observation.

Photographs

There are tens of thousands of photographs of alleged UFOs in existence, but not a single one of them shows an unequivocal UFO clearly, in focus, and in juxtaposition to the ground, buildings or some other reference point. Short of access to an actual UFO, such a photograph would be the most convincing evidence of the existence of UFOs, which explains why so many hoaxers have foisted their wares on the public.

Their efforts were well rewarded in the early days of the UFO era: an excited public accepted as genuine many photographs that later turned out to be faked. As the public grew less excitable, and analytical techniques more sophisticated, it has become less and less easy for a hoaxer to fabricate a photo that will stand up to investigation.

As for those which *do* stand up to analysis, they tend to be short on information content. In an age when almost everyone in the more developed nations possesses a camera, the small proportion of successful photos to sightings is itself a minor phenomenon, causing some ufologists to suggest that UFOs deliberately avoid having their picture taken. Moreover, it seems that the better the photograph, the more dubious the circumstances under which it was taken. The famous Paul Villa photographs, showing a clearly-defined flying saucer in sharp focus, near the ground, in brilliant colour, were taken by Villa alone without a scrap of confirmatory evidence. Adamski's many photographs of scout and mother ships are rendered even more dubious by the contradictions in his account. The sensational series taken at San Juan de Valderes on the outskirts of Madrid in June 1967 demonstrate a contrary process: analysis has shown that the photographs are almost certainly faked, and this has cast suspicion on what might otherwise have been an impressive sighting.[41, 137]

The most common reason for doubting a photograph, though, is simply that it does not tell us enough to convince us it was a UFO and nothing else. After photographing an island off the Welsh coast alleged to be a flying saucer base, I found a curious object on the print. Common sense told me it was a seagull seen in profile, yet it was certainly as good a likeness of a flying saucer as a great many purported UFO photos, and I don't doubt I could have convinced many people I had spotted a UFO returning to its secret base!

However, there are a few photographs which do offer measurable data, and which have stood up successfully to analysis. None is wholly convincing, but at the same time none can reasonably be explained in terms of anything familiar, whether natural or man-made:

McMinnville, Oregon, USA, 11.5.1950 (Case 26). Witness photograph.

Case 26   *McMinnville, Oregon, USA*   *11.5.1950*

Mrs Paul Trent, a country housewife, was feeding her rabbits at about 7.45 pm when she saw a curious object in the sky. 'The object was coming towards us, and seemed to be tipped up a little bit. It was very bright – almost silvery – and there was no noise or smoke. It was not undulating or rotating, just sort of gliding.' She called her husband, who ran to get his camera and managed to take two photographs before the object disappeared into the distance.

The Trents waited until the rest of the film had been used before processing it, and even then they showed the pictures only to a few friends, fearing trouble with the authorities. Eventually a local newspaperman heard of them, and found the negatives under a sofa being played with by the children.[140]

The photographs have been subjected to a great deal of analysis, being re-assessed whenever a new analytical technique is introduced. Sceptics have questioned the Trents' account of how the photographs were taken, but explanations have been plausibly found to account for any discrepancies. A hoax seems ruled out by the fact that elaborate equipment and considerable expertise would be required, and even the Condon Committee (see Chapter 6) discounted the probability. Recent analysis by Ground Saucer Watch, using edge enhancement, colour contouring and digitized image enhancement processes, points to the conclusion that the Trents did indeed photograph a real object, between twenty and thirty metres in diameter and flying at a great distance. The Condon Committee itself admitted that 'this is one of the few UFO reports in which all of the factors investigated, geometrical, psychological, and physical, appear to be consistent with the assertion that an extraordinary flying object, silvery, metallic, disc-shaped, tens of metres in diameter and evidently artificial, flew within sight of two witnesses'.[42]

Case 27   *Namur, Belgium*   *5.6.1955*

M. Muyldermans, a postman, was motoring at 7.30 pm when he noticed a curious object, flying fast but silently. He saw it slow down, and because of its low altitude he thought it was about to land. He stopped and got out of his car for a better look: he could now see that it was disc-shaped, and dark green in colour; sunlight was reflected from a dome on the upper part, and underneath he could see what he took to be landing spheres. Being a photographer, he had his camera with him, and took three photographs. In the first the object was stationary; in the second it had come lower, producing a white vapour trail, and was climbing back through the vapour; in the third it was speeding away, leaving little luminous particles as it went, climbing at a speed Muyldermans estimated at about 500 km/h. The entire observation lasted about 1.5

Namur, Belgium, 5.6.1955 (Case 27). Witness photograph.

minutes, and was positively confirmed by other witnesses. A meteorological expert stated that the vapour trail indicated a minimum   altitude of 1500 metres, and analysis showed the size of the object to be at least twelve metres in diameter.[80]

Case 28   *Trindade Island, Brazil*   *16.1.1958*

The research vessel *Almirante Saldanha* of the Brazilian Navy was preparing to quit Trindade Island where it had been operating, when someone called attention to a strange flying object. Besides the more than a hundred crew members on deck was professional photo-journalist Almiro Barauna, who managed to take four photographs of the object. They showed a disc-shaped object, with a wide flat ring like the planet Saturn. Barauna described the object as dark grey, and seeming to be surrounded by condensation or mist: it moved with a wavelike motion and changed speed abruptly.

Trindade Island, Brazil, 16.1.1958 (Case 28). Witness photograph.

Brazil's Navy Photo Reconnaissance laboratory analysed the negatives and concluded they were genuine. Witnesses

agreed that they matched the object they had seen, and
analyses by two American organizations, APRO and
Ground Saucer Watch, were favourable. Sceptics pointed
out that Barauna was noted for trick photography, and
that he had even produced fake UFO photographs: the
absence of sworn statements by other witnesses, too, is
suspicious. However, it seems improbable that Barauna,
even if he had the facilities, would have perpetrated a
hoax involving the Brazilian Navy.[140]

Hessdalen, Norway, 18.3.1982 (Case 29). Witness photograph.

Case 29   *Hessdalen, Norway*   *18.3.1982*

Over a period of several months, residents of an isolated
country district near Trondheim had reported strange
aerial phenomena. A team of investigators from *UFO
Norge* set up an observation post in the area: they were
rewarded by the sight of some of the phenomena, including
an oval-shaped object manoeuvring and following a
course which took it both in front of and behind hills,
enabling size, distance, altitude and speed to be measured.
Several photographs were obtained which, though they

do not offer much indication of the nature of the objects, provide substantial confirmation that anomalous phenomena were indeed present. Alternative explanations in terms of aircraft or natural phenomena were eliminated.[146]

These cases, and perhaps a handful of others, do seem to offer worthwhile evidence when taken in conjunction with witness accounts. Unfortunately, most of the best UFO cases occur during the hours of darkness, with the result that photography is simply not possible, or, on the rare occasions when photographs have been obtained, the results are ambiguous. As with so much of the physical evidence, the value of photographs seems chiefly to be to confirm visual sightings: in this respect the photographs at Hessdalen (Case 29) and those taken by Harley Rutledge's 'Project Investigation'[131] seem to be the most practically useful.

Other physical effects

There are a great many instances in which various kinds of physical effects from alleged UFOs have been reported. The following case, though bizarre, is by no means unique:

Case 30   Gjersjoen Lake, near Oslo, Norway   11.1953

Trygve Jansen, a commercial painter, was driving with a friend, Fru Gudrun Buflod, when they became aware of a silent flying object, which seemed to be circling round the car, following them. As it came closer they could see that it was disc-shaped with gaseous 'wings', and with a kind of cockpit on top. When it stopped ahead of them on the road, hovering about ten metres above the ground, they were alarmed and Jansen felt compelled to stop also. They sat for about a minute, feeling they were being watched. The object now seemed to be about two metres in diameter, with legs and a dome. Abruptly it took off again and disappeared at great speed: the two witnesses had a prickly feeling, as if they had been exposed to some kind of beam.

When Jansen reached home his wife thought he had a new car, for the dull yellowish beige had turned a beautiful shiny green the colour of verdigris. Unfortunately, by next day the colour was back to normal, but many neighbours had seen the change. Both witnesses felt unwell that evening, Fru Buflod suffering from a paralysed arm. Jansen's watch had stopped and needed expensive repairs: the watchmaker said it had been exposed to a strong magnetic current. Other anomalous lights were seen that evening in Norway.[116]

As long ago as 1960, NICAP was able to publish a report on cases in which electro-magnetic effects seemed to have occurred,[113] and a vast catalogue of such cases could be compiled today. Unfortunately, no constant features have emerged. Some witnesses have approached UFOs without harm, others have been burned even at a considerable distance. Often the effects seem to defy physical laws, as we shall see later (Case 32). While beams of various kinds are very often mentioned, they seem extremely diverse in their effects, to judge by the case of Dr X (Case 18) and that of Betty Cash (Case 23).

Another phenomenon which is frequently claimed to involve vehicles as well as people is teleportation. This was one of the earliest instances:

Case 31   *Near Chascomus, Argentina*   *5.1968*

Senor 'Vidal' (pseudonym) was driving home with his wife late at night, in company with another couple in a separate car, when they drove into thick fog. The next thing they recalled was finding themselves on a dusty, lonely road in daylight. They found that they were in Mexico, some 8000 kilometres distant, and that two days had passed. They went to the Argentina consul in the nearest city; their car was sent to the United States for examination, while they returned to Buenos Aires. Senora Vidal went into hospital, suffering from shock; her husband would make no statement except that he had been instructed to say nothing.[5]

This intriguing case is so unsatisfactory (whatever happened to the car allegedly sent to the US for examination?) as to be utterly worthless as evidence; on the other hand, similar effects have been reported on several occasions – sometimes just of witnesses, sometimes together with their car, on one occasion of a witness on his bicycle! So, while suspending judgement on the phenomenon, it is nevertheless interesting to note that so many witnesses have claimed to experience it.

Case 32   A338 road between Avon and Sopley, England   6.11.1967

Carl Farlow was driving his diesel truck with a load of cookers between 1 and 2 am. Approaching a crossroads near a bridge over the Avon, his lights faded and extinguished. He pulled up with his diesel engine still running, and saw a large egg-shaped object move slowly across the road from his right, about the height of a telegraph pole above the ground: it seemed to be about twenty-five metres in length, covering both the width of the road and the ground to one side as it hovered for a few moments motionless. It was magenta-coloured, with a whitish area at the bottom; it made a sound like a refrigerator, and gave off a smell like a drill boring through wood. After a short while it moved slowly to the left, gradually increasing in speed, and disappeared in a few seconds.

Only then did Farlow notice another car, halted on the far side of the stretch of road traversed by the object. It was a Jaguar, whose driver, a veterinary surgeon, came over to Farlow, explaining that both his engine and his lights were out of action and his girl passenger hysterical. He suggested they telephone the police; fortunately there was a call-box nearby, where the light was out of action but the telephone working. The police arrived shortly afterwards. By the light of the police cars they could see marks on the ground beside the road, and the surface of the road looked as though it had been melted.

The girl was taken to hospital for shock, while the two drivers went to the police station for questioning; they were subsequently taken to the police station at Bournemouth where they were interviewed by a man from the Ministry of Defence.

When the following day Farlow was taken by the police back to the site to collect his belongings from the truck, he saw a swarm of people investigating the site with instruments. A bulldozer was levelling the ground and a man was repainting the telephone kiosk. About a week later, on a subsequent journey, he saw that the road had been resurfaced for about sixty-five metres. £400 worth of damage had been done to the truck: nothing is known about the damage to the Jaguar.[25]

This detailed case is rich in unanswered questions. Much of it suggests a military device of some secret kind, but if so the authorities have successfully kept it secret for a further sixteen years! Whether man-made or extra-terrestrial, the Avon UFO was clearly capable of exerting some very remarkable physical effects; what is disturbing is that these forces do not seem to work in obedience to established principles. To cause even the lights, let alone the engine, to malfunction, would normally call for forces that would inevitably cause substantial external damage in the process: somehow the UFO managed not to do this. Again, while it is conceivable that our scientists are able to operate a 'death-ray' capable of halting a car engine at a distance, it surpasses any technology known to us that the engine could subsequently be re-started without ill-effects. Yet, if witnesses are to be believed, this has happened on several occasions.

The relatively recent exploitation of the microwave effect, whereby – among other things – food can be cooked from the inside out, is a reminder of how much remains to be learned about energy forces. Even without calling into question psychical forces such as psychokinesis, we must accept the possibility of effects beyond anything currently known. At the same time, the discrepancies between the accounts of such effects, as made by UFO witnesses, are so great as to suggest that no single cause is involved. We are faced with a number of one-off cases to which there seems no pattern.

A different kind of reality?

Set beside the tens of thousands of visual sightings of UFOs, the physical evidence is disappointingly meagre. It is as though some primitive tribe, inhabiting some remote corner of the globe, should from time to time see cars hurrying past on purposes incomprehensible to the tribesmen, who have no more immediate proof of their existence than an occasional tyre mark in the dust, some ambiguous damage to vegetation, and the unsubstantiated claims of neighbours to have spoken with the motorists and even to have been given an occasional ride in one.

For many ufologists, this lack of material evidence is an indication that the UFOs are not material by nature. Consequently they look in other directions: some to visual hallucinations and other psychological or even psychical effects, others to non-material forms visiting us from alternate planes of reality. Such alternatives certainly merit consideration, and there can be no question that whatever the UFOs are, they demand a new and open-minded approach to reality such as that long demanded by ghosts and other paranormal phenomena. Yet we have seen that there is sufficient evidence to suggest that UFOs do possess a physical dimension. And if so, for us who inhabit a physical universe, this may still be our most practicable access point, even though we shall eventually have to come to terms with the non-physical dimensions of the phenomenon.

FOUR: THE UFO WITNESS

Our brief survey of the physical evidence for UFOs makes it clear that the evidence is only as good as the witness who provides it. Radar returns depend on radar operators, photographs depend on the photographer. Certainly it is not easy to suppose that truck driver Farlow (Case 32) would deliberately damage his vehicle in order to fake a UFO story; but he might conceivably fake a UFO story in order to explain damage from some other cause. Similarly, while it is hard to imagine why forestry worker Taylor (Case 4) should go to such trouble to fake the puzzling marks associated with his alleged sighting, our evaluation of them will depend on our evaluation of *him*.

The vast bulk of UFO evidence has no such material support; it consists simply of eyewitness accounts by people who are unable to explain what they have seen. Generally, they do their best to find explanations. Eugene Coquil (Case 2) assumed at first he was seeing a tractor; M. Masse (Case 6) thought in terms of a helicopter; the Hills (Case 17) took their UFO for an airliner. Only when these conventional explanations proved inadequate did they start to think in terms of 'one of those flying saucer things'. Even then, witnesses are liable to fit the UFO into their belief system: religious people, for whom the existence of benevolent spirits is a matter of everyday belief, will so interpret their sighting. Thus in March 1967 a mother and daughter from Letart Falls, California, were driving home from church late one night when they encountered a bizarre creature in the road with long hair and white wings about three metres wide – one of many

sightings in the UFO-related 'mothman' flap. Being very
devout, the witnesses assumed they had seen an angel, if
not Jesus Christ in person.[86] On the other hand, Betty
Cash (Case 23) continues to maintain that the UFO which
burned her face was something man-made, no doubt a
secret military device.

In short, witness response is conditioned by personal
attitude, which will in turn be conditioned by cultural
background. The immediate circumstances will provide
an additional modifying factor. It will be up to the
investigator to assess the part played by such factors in a
case like the following:

Case 33   *Langford Budville, Somerset, England*   16.10.1973

An anonymous West Country woman, aged forty-three,
was driving along a country road at about 11 pm when her
engine and lights ceased to function. She got out to see
what was wrong, and felt something touch her: she turned
to see a robot-like figure behind her, some two metres
tall, and promptly fainted. When she came to her senses,
she and the robot were standing beside a domed vehicle,
about six metres long and twelve metres high: she
promptly fainted again. When she next came to she was
tied naked onto a metallic table inside the ship, in a
colourless room whose walls glowed eerily. Three human-
like figures, a little less than two metres tall, conducted a
physical examination of her; then two of them left and
the third assaulted her sexually. She was terrified and
wanted to scream but her throat was sore: she fainted yet
again. When she came to she was back in her car, and
three hours had passed. She was able to start the car, and
drove home where she told her husband and eventually
informed the police.[51]

The similarity of this case to that of the Hills and many
others can be interpreted in various ways. We may
conclude that she fantasized the episode, subconsciously
utilizing for the purpose her memories of reading such

accounts; or we may suppose that this is a genuine experience which a considerable number of people in various parts of the world are undergoing. Given the inherent improbability of the incident, and the total lack of supporting evidence, it might seem preferable to attribute the report to the witness' imagination, in which case it should not be too difficult to diagnose her unconscious motivation. But this is by no means to relegate the case to the files of psychopathology: the proliferation of such reports must, in any case, be seen as both significant and alarming.

Case 34   *Broadhaven, Wales*   *10.1977*

Mrs Pauline Coombes, a farmer's wife, was driving home with her family in the late afternoon along a country side road, when they saw an object streak over their car. They stopped, and watched the object dive into the side of a rocky island off the coast, where huge concealed doors in the rock face seemed to slide apart to allow the machine to enter. Along with the journalist who wrote a book about her experiences, she took this as evidence that UFOs were using the island as a base.[74, 117, 47]

Unlike the journalist, a BBC reporter visited the island and established that, in fact, there is no secret UFO base there. What the witness reported, then, is either fiction or hallucination. Giving her the benefit of the doubt, we could suppose that she had seen a bird or an aircraft flying towards the island, and had 'manufactured' the rest in her head. Admittedly the psychological process is complex, and its motivation obscure: but the literature of hallucination is sufficiently rich to demonstrate that this kind of thing can and does occur (see, for example [20]). Experienced ufologists learn to look out for details that seem to be suggested by what we may term the currently prevailing folklore – which today means all the apparatus of science fiction and space travel, including encounters with aliens and UFO bases on off-shore islands.

Given a personal predisposition on the witness' part, and an appropriate scenario offered by the prevailing folklore, an imaginary UFO experience can be triggered by social contagion. Some such process was surely operating on a national scale in France in the autumn of 1954, when several such cases as the following occurred:

Case 35   *Sinceny, Aisne, France*   *10.1954*

A Monsieur F. reported: 'Seeing a silhouette moving in the light of two lamps, I thought I was in the presence of a Martian in the process of repairing his flying saucer. I went to get my gun and I fired at him.' It turned out to be a neighbour, M. Maurice R., repairing his motor car in a nearby field. Fortunately, F.'s shot only damaged the car.[30]

Ideally, no doubt, every witness should be subjected to a detailed psychological test, but only in exceptional cases is this practicable. The investigator must simply do his best to take into account the diverse distorting factors which may be operating, bearing in mind that more than one factor may be combining to create the error:

Case 36   *Snowflake, Arizona, USA*   *15.11.1975*

Two men were hunting in a forest area; about 3 am they were driving home when they saw a brilliant light in the distance, which seemed to come up above the level of the trees and position itself ahead of them on the road. They stopped, and the object, which was completely silent, stopped also. As they drove on, it kept its distance over a period of two or three hours, though gradually increasing its altitude. Looked at through a rifle sight, the object seemed as though it might be saucer-shaped, but was too bright to be seen clearly. Worried and excited, they reached home and one witness woke his wife who confirmed the sighting.

Investigators established, beyond doubt, that the hunters had simply seen the planet Venus. Perhaps the visual conditions were exceptionally conducive to error, but what surely contributed most to the misidentification was the fact that, just ten days earlier, a particularly sensational UFO incident, the alleged abduction of forest worker Travis Walton, had taken place only five kilometres from where the two men were hunting.[133]

In the absence of such special circumstances, UFO witnesses have on the whole shown themselves to be reliable in *reporting* what they see. An especially noteworthy instance was the following:

Case 37 *Over Southampton, England* *4.1979*

An agency report from Southampton stated that passengers who had reported seeing, from the windows of their aircraft, an orange coloured elephant flying among the clouds, were not victims of a hallucination. What they had seen, and accurately described, was a balloon in the shape of an elephant, which had been used to publicize a circus but had broken loose and soared to more than 12,000 metres![127]

Patterns of predisposition

Attempts have been made to trace patterns in UFO witnesses, to establish that certain categories of people are more likely than others to have sightings. In particular, it has been proposed that people of a psychic disposition are particularly prone to UFO experiences. Another across-the-board suggestion is the 'status-inconsistency' hypothesis, which Donald I. Warren proposed in 1970. After studying a Gallup poll on UFO percipients, he produced figures to show that people who suffer from status inconsistency – that is, who earn a lot more or less than their educational qualifications suggest – are more likely to see a UFO. He concluded that 'UFOs provide a form of escape into unrealized and perhaps unrealizable situations'.[157]

Any such finding, if proved sound, would require us to

re-evaluate our statistics. So perhaps it is just as well that no intelligent ufologist would in any case place much reliance on such statistics as are presently available. Gathered from so many different sources, over so long a time period, the level of investigation is inevitably uneven; factors stressed by some will have been neglected by others: lack of data, as in our Case 74, invalidates other cases. Most cases in most UFO catalogues must be regarded as of little more than anecdotal value.

This does not mean that such cases are necessarily false. For what is reassuring about the catalogues is that they show the great majority of cases as generally consistent one with another, the weak with the strong, and the single-witness cases with those that are supported by additional testimony.

The pragmatic approach

Ideally, no doubt, we would not accept a single UFO report until we had obtained a comprehensive profile of the witness – his psychological make-up, his socio-cultural background, his economic status and so forth, to which we would add an assessment of the social factors prevailing at the time – the level of UFO activity as reported in the media, current attitudes and the like. Since, however, this state of perfection can be attained only in a minute fraction of cases, the question arises, to what extent should any witness' statement be accepted?

The cases we have already examined in this chapter make one thing clear: the necessity of distinguishing between believing the *witness* and believing *what the witness says*. This is illustrated by the following case:

Case 38   *Herbrandston, Wales*   *14.4.1977*

Thirteen-year-old Debbie Swan told investigators that she was with a group of other children in a public park at 6.30 pm. Since many UFO reports had lately been circulating in the neighbourhood, they decided to see if they could find this 'outer space thing', but having gone a little way from the park, two of them turned back because 'it began to get scary'. The others went on, under fences, across a potato field, down a bank, and then: 'There was something in a field opposite out of the ordinary. I have never seen anything like it before in my life ... I thought it was my eyes playing a trick, but it wasn't. The most astonishing thing about it was the colour, which was a brilliant gleaming silver. It moved at all angles – backwards, frontwards, left to right: as we moved, it moved as well. We ran back as fast as we could . . . '[26]

Now it is simply without precedent for anyone to go out looking for UFOs and to run into one in the first five minutes. Most ufologists have been looking vainly for years for a sight of a UFO! That consideration alone should have put investigators on their guard: yet Debbie's story was unquestioningly accepted by virtually everyone investigating the sightings. A more critical attitude would have accepted that she may well have been perfectly sincere, but suspected that she had been conditioned by the recent excitement into a state of expectancy; her imagination did the rest. What is alarming about that case is not so much that Debbie Swan made her claim but that it was accepted at face value by supposedly competent investigators.

During that same Welsh flap, a group of schoolchildren claimed to see a UFO in a field near their school, where it remained for more than three hours in full daylight and in full view of several houses. Again, this fact alone – which would make the case unique in UFO literature – should of itself have been sufficient to arouse the suspicions of the investigators: but here again, because the witnesses were evidently sincere, their story was accepted at face value.

Clearly, sincerity is not enough. When a woman in her 40s claims to have been raped by a spaceman, as in Case 33, but can produce no evidence to support her assertion, we are surely justified in suspecting that her conscious statement echoes a subconscious fear, or wish, rather than an actual occurrence. With the following case we can afford to be more accepting but should still be sceptical:

Case 39   Blenheim, New Zealand   13.7.1959

Mrs Moreland, a nurse who also helped her husband with his farm, went out just before 6 am to do the morning milking and noticed a green glow in the pre-dawn sky. She was halfway across the paddock when she saw two large green lights emerge from low clouds: taking refuge beneath some trees, she saw a saucer-shaped object with two occupants, which descended and hovered about five metres above the ground at a distance of some fifty metres or less.[114]

In the following case, however, there seems no reason not be accept the witness' statement as it stands:

Case 40   Idaho Falls, USA   8.12.1967

Marilyn Wilding, aged fifteen, was out on the front step of her home, waiting for a friend to pick her up at about 7.40 pm, when she became aware of a strange illumination in the sky. Stepping further out, she saw a large brightly lit circular object hovering not far above the house. As she watched, it tilted and she could see that it contained two figures. Her brothers and sisters, as well as some neighbours, confirmed the sighting.[114]

This case also illustrates the consistency factor, for it closely resembles many other sightings, including our Cowichan Hospital case (Case 5). The fact that one case resembles another proves nothing: consistency is a two-edged argument. When a witness reports seeing something very like what others have seen, it could mean:

* both have seen similar objects;
* both have imagined or hallucinated similar objects; or

* one is deliberately or subconsciously modelling his story on the other.

When two witnesses report differing objects, it could mean:

* each has seen a different object;
* each has imagined or hallucinated a different object; or
* one is deliberately describing a different object to make his story more believable.

However, in cases where it is unlikely that the second witness will be familiar with the earlier sighting, consistency encourages belief, as does the fact that accounts given by experienced pilots, astronomers and engineers are very similar to those given us by housewives and working men, and that those seen in one part of the world are very much like those seen in another.

*   *   *   *

In this chapter we have considered some of the aspects of UFO reports that might make us hesitant to accept them at face value. But once those aspects have been allowed for, it seems reasonable to proceed on the assumption that the majority of witnesses not only believe they are telling the truth, but *are* telling the truth. Because some paintings are forgeries, it does not follow that all are: there have to be originals for which the forgeries can be mistaken. So with UFO reports, though we may have reason to suspect that some are deliberate hoaxes or sincerely narrated subconscious recollections of others' experiences, it seems legitimate to adopt a pragmatic approach, and see what we can learn by taking eyewitness accounts at face value unless we have good reason to doubt their reliability.

FIVE: THE VISUAL EVIDENCE

Eyewitness accounts of sightings are the heart of the UFO evidence. Consequently, it is essential for us to recognize that the vast majority of these witnesses – who show no sign of being any less sane, honest and intelligent than the rest of us – believed they were seeing physical objects, real and substantial.

This is so fundamental a fact that it is easily overlooked. But in formulating alternative hypotheses – that what the witness saw was a psychic projection triggered by a geophysical phenomenon, for example – we must have good grounds for setting aside the assertion of the witness himself. As McCampbell insists in his classic study, 'until another hypothesis has been shown to be more productive, UFO reports should be considered as sincere attempts by people to describe personal experiences, no matter how bizarre they seem'.[98] From which this corrollary surely follows: that until another explanation has been shown to be more compatible with the facts, the explanation given by the witness should be accorded priority. Often, of course, the witness himself is at a loss for an explanation; but at least our interpretation should aim at making sense of his account, not at squeezing and trimming it to fit a predetermined pigeonhole.

1. What the objects are

Descriptions of UFOs fall into two basic categories. Those that have no discernible shape other than an amorphous 'blob', and that have been conjectured to be natural phenomena of some kind unknown to current science; and those that possess a structured shape, suggesting fabrication by someone, somewhere.

a. UFOs as natural phenomena

Case 41   *Hebron, Maryland, USA*   *16.7.1952*

Two state policemen, Robert Burkhardt and his sergeant, were on patrol around midnight. They were travelling along a tree-lined road when they saw a yellow light ahead heading straight for their patrol car; they assumed it to be either a motorcycle or a car with one defective headlamp. As it came directly towards them, they swerved onto the shoulder of the road and halted. The globe of light also halted, hovering in the beam of their lights, about six metres ahead. Burkhardt moved his car slowly forward: as he did so, the light retreated. When he varied his speed, the light maintained its distance. Finally, the light disappeared with a burst of speed. The phenomenon was repeated on other occasions and witnessed by several others.[75]

No structured shape was seen, nothing to suggest what we commonly think of as a UFO. Judging by appearance alone, the light has more in common with the will-of-the-wisp of folklore and the various 'spook lights' reported from different parts of the world. Clearly, it is tempting to ascribe these to natural causes such as gaseous exhalations; but how is this to be reconciled with the seemingly intelligent behaviour?

Case 42   *New Jersey, USA*   *25.9.1965*

Author and biologist Ivan Sanderson was driving with a colleague after sunset when they saw a red light to the right of Venus and much brighter than the planet, at low altitude in a clear sky. It was flashing – not pulsing – on and off. As they watched, it divided into two portions which moved apart in opposite directions, both red and both flashing about twice per second. One disappeared behind trees: the other performed a series of manoeuvres, including abrupt angular turns, at a speed estimated at many thousands of km/h.[34]

This is a classic 'lights-in-the-sky' observation, made noteworthy by the fact that the observer was a well-known biologist with a special interest in anomalous phenomena. As a biologist, Sanderson was aware of the immense diversity of natural species and considered it possible that many UFOs are intelligent life-forms.

Such speculations have been made from the earliest days of the UFO era. In 1947, the same year as Kenneth Arnold's sighting, John Philip Bessor tried to persuade the US Air Force that flying saucers were 'various species of extraterrestrial, highly attenuated life-forms or craft propelled by telekinetic energy or by sheer will or thought. Possibly originating in the ionosphere, they have been forced to "migrate" to denser atmospheres periodically because of solar or cosmic disturbances. They are capable of changing shape in flight and possess the intelligence of the octopus, porpoise or chimpanzee.'[15]

Case 43   Mojave Desert, California, USA   25.8.1957 etc

New Zealander Trevor James Constable obtained a number of photographs using infra-red film, which showed shapeless blobs in the lower atmosphere. He identified these as natural creatures inhabiting our air-space but normally invisible.[38]

Constable's efforts have not been satisfactorily replicated, and so have only the slightest evidential value. But it must be remembered that we possess an enormous number of cases in which the phenomenon is described simply as an amorphous blob of light, possessing nothing to suggest an artificial structure, yet behaving in a manner that suggests intelligent control. The Foo Fighters of World War Two (Case 9) are an obvious example.

While some theorists hold to an organic explanation,

others, noting the similarity of such lights to those seen immediately prior to earthquake activity, for example, look to some kind of plasma, created by geophysical forces. Another alternative is meteorological phenomena: something akin to ball lightning has been proposed[91] and Steuart Campbell, investigator of the Livingston case (Case 4), has suggested that some form of ball lightning may have been at work in this instance.

Few ufologists would claim that such explanations can account for the entire spectrum of UFO sightings; but if they could be shown to account for a proportion, it would simplify the problem of accounting for the rest.

b. UFOs as structured artefacts

Most people who report seeing UFOs, apart from simple lights and blobs, describe them as having some kind of structured shape; they look as if they have been *built* – which, of course, implies builders.

To say that UFOs come in literally all shapes and sizes is hardly an exaggeration. From time to time enthusiasts have tried to compile charts of the various types, but the sheer variety has proved too much for them; and such an effort carries the danger that an inconvenient feature will be 'overlooked' to make the object fit an existing category. It is closer to the truth to say that virtually no UFO can be said for certain to be identical to any other. This is in itself a significant fact, seized upon by debunkers and those who favour non-physical explanations. But to say that UFOs are too varied to be true is to argue from premises that may not be valid. The diversity of models of motorcars on Earth might well be equally puzzling to an alien visitor: if UFOs should turn out to be extraterrestrial in origin, it would be premature for us to make any judgement based on human logic.

In any case, despite the diversity of types, several do recur. Disc-shaped objects are probably the most prevalent: there are discs large and small, smooth or domed. Frequently they possess rotating rings, often illuminated, and this has given encouragement to engineers who have amused themselves and us by speculating on possible propulsion systems. Here is a disc sighting with particularly impressive confirmation:

Case 44   Exeter, New Hampshire, USA   3.9.1965

Eighteen-year-old Norman Muscarello was hitchhiking home, some time after midnight, but due to lack of traffic was having to walk the last part of his journey. Nearing Exeter he saw, over an open field and between two houses, a 'thing' of about thirty metres diameter, with brilliant pulsating red lights round an apparent rim. It wobbled as it floated silently towards him; when it seemed as if it was going to hit him, he drove into the shallow shoulder of the road. It then seemed to back off slowly, and Muscarello ran to one of the houses, pounding on the door but getting no response. He then managed to get a lift into Exeter, where he reported his experience at the police station in a state of extreme nervousness. While hesitating what to make of his story, the police learnt from a patrolman of a woman he'd found parked in her car, shaken by seeing something very similar. A police officer went back to the site with Muscarello and had a clear view of the object enabling him to confirm the sighting totally; partial confirmation was obtained from another patrol car which saw the object but not in such detail.[60]

Cone-shapes, bell-shapes, cigar-shapes – these too are recurring forms. Mention should also be made of one recurring pattern, first described by Adamski[2] and echoed by others, which claims to detect the existence of two basic types of craft: the interstellar type, popularly known as a 'mother ship', and a smaller craft operating tactically within our planet's atmosphere, known as a 'scout ship'. Here is a well confirmed sighting:

Case 45   Vernon, France   22-23.8.1954

M. Miserey, a businessman, returned home after midnight,

and was putting his car away when he had a sense of something unusual: he realized that the town, totally dark a moment ago, was bathed in a pale light. Looking up, he saw a huge cigar-shaped object, hovering vertically about 300 metres over the north bank of the river. After staring at it for a moment he saw a smaller object detach from it: this was a horizontal disc-shape which at first seemed to drop in free fall, then slowed, and suddenly rocked and headed in his direction, becoming very bright. It vanished behind him at great speed. After a few moments he saw a second, similar, object detach from the lower end of the 'cigar', behaving in the same way; then a third and a fourth. Finally, after an interval, a fifth disc dropped lower than the others, almost touching the bridge, and hovered for a moment wobbling, enabling M. Miserey to see its circular shape, with a red luminosity which was more intense at the centre and less so at the rim, and also the surrounding halo. After a few seconds this disc, too, made off, but in an opposite direction from the others. Meanwhile the 'cigar', which he estimated as about 100 metres long, lost its brightness and faded into the darkness. All in all, the observation lasted some 45 minutes. The following day M. Miserey informed the police, and learnt that his sighting had been shared by two policemen in a patrol car and also by an engineer, M. Millet.[64]

The case is by no means unique. On 17 September 1966, for example, Mr and Mrs Rogers of Ipswich, Massachusetts, watched an almost identical display, with the added bonus that they saw the smaller objects leave and rejoin the larger one several times.[57] Another mother-and-scout case presents us with a particularly baffling mystery:

Case 46   Palomar Gardens, California, USA   13.12.1952

George Adamski, who a month before had met with a Venusian in the desert (Case 12), had a return visit by the Venusian in his scout ship. Adamski had time to take a

few photographs through a camera attached to his telescope, as the ship hovered 100 to 150 metres over the
valley. Then it flew away, being seen and photographed
by other witnesses whom Adamski, expecting such a visit,
had previously alerted.[95]

Palomar Gardens, California, USA, 13.12.1952 (Case 46). Witness
photograph.

Subsequently, while being taken on a space voyage by his contacts, Adamski was able to photograph the 'mother' ships also. Besides the inherent improbability of his story, his account contains many exaggerations and untruths, as well as factual errors, and this has made most ufologists reluctant to accept his story though he still has many loyal adherents. What encourages his followers, and dismays his critics, is an episode such as the following:

Case 47   *Coniston, England*   *15.2.1954*

Thirteen-year-old Stephen Darbishire went up on the hill behind his home one morning, with his eight-year-old cousin Adrian, hoping to photograph birds. About 11 am Adrian pointed out a strange object in the sky, which Stephen photographed. He thought his camera was set to infinity but it was not, so the pictures came out blurred. Nevertheless, they showed what he claimed to have seen, 'a solid metal-like thing, with a dome, portholes, and three bumps or landing domes underneath'. Stephen's father was sceptical, but got his son to write down a description; the film was taken to a man in the village with a photographic studio, who telephoned to say 'There's something on it and it looks like a flying saucer'. In fact, the object Stephen had photographed was shown by ufologist Leonard Cramp to be identical with the scout ship photographed by Adamski.[40]

According to Desmond Leslie, whose book *Flying Saucers Have Landed*[95] contained the first account of Adamski's adventures, Adamski's negatives were examined by Pev Marley, a Hollywood expert in trick photography, who declared that if they were fakes, they were the best he had ever seen. A model aircraft manufacturer was convinced the photographs were not of models but of objects ten metres in diameter.

Numerous allegations were made that Adamski had actually used a terrestrial object as his model: a chicken brooder was the most favoured suggestion. But nobody has yet produced a chicken-brooder that precisely matches his photographs: this would seem to be the minimum requirement for invalidating his pictures. Similarly, the Darbishire photographs have yet to be proved false.

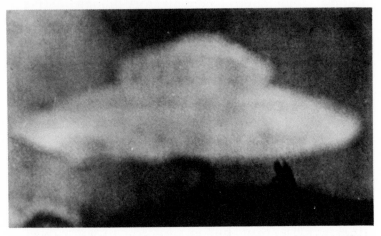

Coniston, England, 15.2.1954 (Case 47). Witness photograph.

So we are faced with two sets of photographs, both of them suspiciously out of focus, both taken by (virtually) solitary individuals without any supporting evidence whatsoever, yet showing the same object. Supposing that Adamski *did* employ a chicken-brooder, how did thirteen-year-old Stephen in England get hold of an identical object, or manufacture a facsimile, and photograph it in such a way as to stand up to analysis?

To add to the dilemma, the Darbishire photo is by no means the only Adamski replica: Hugo Vega photographed a similar object in Peru on 19.10.1973, and so did W. D. Hall in Australia in the same year as the Darbishire photograph.[93] If we could be sure that none, or one, or some, or all these witnesses are faking, it would be a major step towards solving the UFO enigma.

Though the fact that witnesses tend to report similar objects can be seen as corroboration, then, it can also suggest plagiarism. So, paradoxically, it may be more convincing when accounts differ: and among the thousands of reports there is certainly scope for a wide range.

Case 48   *Menton, France*   *1.1964*

A retired scientist saw, and touched, a metallic disc, very thin, joined without seam to a sphere forming a dome above and a kind of flat-bottomed bowl beneath.[97]

Case 49   *Laborie, France*   *20.11.1979*

M. and Mme Michelet saw a diamond-shaped object in the night sky, with a light at each corner. Three were red and one orange, but the red lights turned orange in clockwise succession. The witnesses could see nothing but the lights, but they seemed fixed in relation to one another, suggesting they were part of a structure.[97]

Case 50   *Trans-en-Provence, France*   *8.1.1981*

M. Nicolai saw a plain disc, like a flat soup-bowl, upturned on top of another, standing on four short legs on the ground; it left marks.[97]

Case 51   *Seignes, France*   *24.10.1978*

A motorist encountered a sphere, about four metres in diameter, hovering over the road ahead of him. It was luminous and rotating anti-clockwise, while a band of 'infra-red' at the centre rotated clockwise.[97]

Case 52   *Sturno, Italy*   *31.8.1977*

Seven witnesses saw a vertical cylinder on the ground, with alternating bright and dark stripes and a domed top; they also saw an entity with it.[56]

Case 53   *Monreal del Campo, Spain*   *9.3.1969*

Sr. and Sra. Mira, medical students, were driving from Valencia to Zaragoza when they saw, about two kilometres distant, an object like a flattened egg, with a smaller white sphere floating alongside. The 'egg' had six luminous points in its central part, emitting various flashes as it landed vertically. Later the witnesses saw the same or a similar object in flight.[7]

Canary Islands, 22.6.1976 (Case 54). Artist's impression.

Case 54   *Canary Islands*   *22.6.1976*

A number of sightings were made of this UFO as it passed from the island of Fuerteventura via Gran Canaria towards Tenerife. It was first seen as a ball of light, which then began to project a beam: it covered the distance from one island to the next at over 3000 km/h. On Gran Canaria a doctor, in a taxi with three others on the way to visit a patient, saw a gigantic ball, electric blue in colour, hanging stationary about two metres above the ground at a distance of some fifty metres. They watched for nearly twenty minutes, seeing two very tall entities inside a sphere that was like an enormous soap bubble with a diameter comparable to a two-floor house. When the cab driver turned his spotlight on the object, it rose and swelled, though the entities and the objects inside the vessel remained the same size: eventually it was the size of a twenty-storey house. The witnesses fled to a nearby house but watched from a window. Suddenly the object gave a high pitched whistle and shot away towards Tenerife. As it went its shape changed to that of a spindle, surrounded by a big vivid white halo. Many other witnesses saw the object which was also detected on radar and photographed, though the photos show only an enigmatic luminous object.[12]

We could continue to cite such cases ad infinitum; but, together with others referred to in this book, they surely establish that witnesses are observing an extraordinary variety of objects, about which little more can be said than that they give evidence of being designed and fabricated, and exhibit intelligence – up to a point – in the way they behave. Evidently this diversity of shape is not accidental, but somehow meaningful: but the meaning continues to elude rational analysis. Some of the shapes, like that of Case 48, make aerodynamic sense, while others, like Case 52, clearly do not. We can understand some of the features, like the landing 'legs' of Case 50, while others, such as the flashing coloured lights of Case 49, seem utterly nonsensical. Above all, the capability of the objects to divide and rejoin, as in Case 45, and to change shape and size, as in Cases 54 and 58, appears to defy physical laws as we at present understand them.

2. What the UFOs do

Case 55   *Mt Rainier, Washington, USA*   *24.6.1947*

Kenneth Arnold, an experienced civilian pilot, was flying his private plane in a mountain district when, about 3 pm, a bright flash directed his attention to nine flying objects rapidly approaching Mount Rainier. They were flying as separate objects in a close formation and seemed to skim through the air, as Arnold himself expressed it, 'like flying saucers'. It seemed to him that the speed of the objects was more than 2500 km/h; even if he grossly overestimated it, this was far more than could be achieved by any aircraft of the day.[6]

It was this sighting that hit the world's headlines and so ushered in the present UFO era. From the outset, it was above all the high speeds attained by the UFOs that most impressed the public; other aspects of their behaviour were open to various interpretations, but speed is absolute and measurable. If an object flies faster than anything known to man, its strangeness is beyond question. In the post-war climate of 1947, the idea that there existed anything capable of flying that fast was alarming to the American authorities, who naturally feared lest the Russians had stolen a march on them. However, it was soon apparent that there was more to the UFOs than their turn of speed. There was also their ability to accelerate from a 'standing start':

Case 56   Silver City, New Mexico, USA   mid 8. 1951

At 10.30 in the morning mining engineer Alford Roos saw from his ranch two lens-shaped UFOs manoeuvring, hovering and moving in various ways. At one point, he saw them move 'from almost stationary to instant about 800 km/h'. As he pointed out, the shock of inertia would make it impossible for any human to survive such a degree of acceleration. Several other witnesses confirmed his testimony.[73]

Abrupt turns were another speciality:

Case 57   Lincoln, Nebraska, USA   6.10.1959

A Colonel reported how he, his wife and their son had watched a luminous spherical object dart about in the night sky. Moving at a speed that seemed to the witnesses to be much faster than that of a jet plane, it made several abrupt changes of direction, including two ninety-degree turns. After about two minutes it faded from sight.[116]

Although it was generally believed at that time that the UFOs must be somebody's spacecraft, extraterrestrial or otherwise, it was the apparent impossibility of such manoeuvres that set the more thoughtful ufologists looking for alternative explanations, and this was reinforced by shape-changing cases such as the following:

Case 58   *Over Labrador, Canada*   *29.6.1954*

James Howard was in command of a BOAC Stratocruiser on the New York to London run. He had left New York but had been diverted for a while (no reason being given) from his normal flight path; while there is no indication that this was connected with his subsequent sighting, the possibility must be kept in mind. Some three hours after leaving New York he and his crew became aware of a group of UFOs that seemed to be accompanying the aircraft, though maintaining a distance of some five kilometres. There were seven objects, one large and six small: though flying together, the pattern varied – at times three might be preceding the larger object, at other times four, and so on. They were travelling at the same speed as the aircraft, of course, some 600 km/h: their altitude was lower at first, then about the same level. The objects flew with the aircraft for about twenty minutes, during which time they were seen by all the crew and several of the passengers. They were grey, opaque, hard-edged, and without lights. The large object was continually changing its shape, sometimes appearing as clearly defined as an aircraft, at others quite shapeless.[56]

This was one of the cases selected for consideration by the Condon Committee of 1966, whose work we shall be noting in the next chapter. Clearly baffled by the case, they concluded with these remarkable words, which rather suggest that their author had his tongue in his cheek when he wrote them: 'This unusual sighting should therefore be assigned to the category of some almost certainly natural phenomenon which is so rare that it apparently has never been reported before or since.'[37]

The shape-changing is certainly easiest to reconcile with some kind of natural phenomenon, but it is not easy to conceive that it would be sustained over a distance of more than 150 kilometres. Again, the fact that the objects maintained more or less the same position relative to the observing aircraft would suggest a meteorological phenomenon; but how is this to be reconciled with the changing positions of the smaller and larger objects?

The BOAC witnesses had the advantage that theirs was a daylight sighting: the military observers in the following case lacked that advantage, but had the compensating benefit of radar confirmation:

Case 59   South and central United States   17.5.1957

A United States RB-47 bomber, with a crew of six, was on the return leg of a training flight, during which exercises were carried out using various equipment including ECM (Electronic Countermeasures). At 4.10 am local time, visual contact was made with a luminous object, which proceeded to accompany the bomber for the ensuing 1.5 hours, during which time the aircraft flew more than 1200 kilometres from the Gulf of Mexico over several states to Forbes Air Force Base in Kansas. It was flying not a straight but a very indirect course, including at one stage a complete loop. The object was seen at various times by the cockpit crew; it was detected by the ECM monitoring gear on the plane; and it was followed by ground radar alerted by the bomber. Several of these observations were simultaneous, and specific incidents, such as the appearance or disappearance of the object, were detected by all three means. The object displayed a remarkable rapidity of manoeuvre, including abrupt shifts from starboard to port of the bomber and back again. Though seen for the most part as 'a huge light', the commander had a distinct impression that the light emanated from the top of an unseen object.

The fact that the object was seen in different directions, not only as the aircraft itself changed course but also relative to the aircraft itself, rules out any explanation in terms of reflections, or misinterpretations of celestial objects, ground lights, etc. The instrumental confirmation eliminates visual error and vice versa. The combined evidence clearly indicates a physical object, with some degree of intelligence, capable of outflying and out-manoeuvring an aircraft over considerable periods.[132]

The foregoing case includes a frequently reported characteristic of UFOs: an ability to appear from 'nowhere' and to vanish equally abruptly. Here is a particularly vivid example:

Case 60   Nouatre, near Marcilly-sur-Vienne, France   30.9.1954

Georges Gatay was working in a quarry with a team of eight stone-workers, of which he was foreman. About 4.30 pm he had a strange physical sensation of torpor, and suddenly found himself confronted by a little being about 1.5 metres tall, standing in front of an object some 4.5 metres in diameter. Its shape was a shining dome, hovering about a metre above the ground, with blades like a helicopter's. He tried to run, but found himself paralyzed: his fellow-workers, too, were unable to move for about thirty seconds. Then the entity disappeared, and the machine took off with a loud whistling sound; it rose in a series of leaps to a height of about 200 metres, then vanished in a kind of blue cloud.[70]

If such accounts can be trusted, there is virtually no limit to what the UFOs are potentially capable of. There is no need to assume that all the various types have the same capability: it may be that some can do some things, some others. But if so, no patterns are evident. Each event seems to be as much a one-off occasion as the objects themselves appear to be one-off objects. Somehow, whatever explanation we come up with has got to take this diversity of behaviour into account along with the diversity of appearance.

3. Who controls the objects?

Many, perhaps most, UFOs behave in ways that indicate intelligence. If they are natural phenomena, they may possess a degree of intelligence of their own: if artefacts, they may house intelligent beings or be under intelligent control.

Many UFOs seem to be no more than small luminous spheres that do not seem large enough to contain other beings; however, we must not assume too much – a spaceship crewed by intelligent ants, for example, would need to be no larger than a tennis ball, so that even a Foo Fighter (Case 9) could contain a crew. Equally, they might be under remote control from distant sources that guide them with the help of monitors.

However, it is well enough established that most UFOs whose size has been calculated are of 'human' scale and in cases where occupants have been observed, they are, if not of our stature, then not far from it. Only very rarely, and not in well-authenticated cases, have beings been observed of a totally different order of dimension, such as little men a few centimetres tall. (For notes on very tall occupants see[85], for very small ones see[119].)

We have now hundreds of cases on record in which witnesses claim to have observed UFO occupants, either in the craft or emerging from or entering them. This has encouraged researchers to attempt a classification of the various species. The results are very similar to attempts to classify the UFOs themselves: that is to say, a disconcerting diversity of types has been reported, but a few salient species seem to predominate. French ufologist Eric Zurcher[161] has analysed them closely, and found that:

* some 20 per cent are more or less human, including an important sub-group of beautiful males with long hair;

* some 34 per cent are little bipeds with large heads;

* some 5 per cent are hairy bipeds;

* some 30 per cent are not seen distinctly because they are wearing 'space suits' or something of the sort.

The balance is made up of other types, more or less bizarre, including giants, miniature creatures, and entities that have nothing at all human about them.

That a majority of UFO occupants should be more or less humanoid is improbable, if we take them to be extraterrestrials, for the chances of life developing on such similar lines on another planet are reckoned to be small. Even more improbable is the fact that most UFO occupants are reported as moving under our gravity conditions and breathing our atmosphere without much difficulty (though there are a few cases that suggest they may be experiencing problems of adjustment). That the physical conditions of Earth should be duplicated elsewhere is statistically most unlikely.

Such reasoning for a long time discouraged researchers from taking occupant reports, and contact stories in particular, seriously. They still constitute formidable obstacles to the extraterrestrial hypothesis, and have encouraged the champions of the alternative explanations we shall be looking at in Chapter 7. One thing is certain, however: trustworthy witnesses continue to report cases like the following, and we cannot exclude their observations from the rest of the testimony.

Case 61   *Near Figueras, Spain*   *10.1958*

Senor Angelu, a forty-year-old businessman, was riding his motorcycle about 7 pm when he saw an object fall from the sky and seem to crash in a wood. Thinking to help, he went to the scene, and saw not a crashed but a landed object – a classic UFO shape resembling a plate inverted on another, with a transparent cockpit on top and standing on legs, the overall diameter being about eight metres. He could see a figure in the cockpit, and two more were on the ground outside: they were human in appearance but only about one metre tall, with over-large heads. They were moving about and gathering something from the ground; then they rejoined their ship, which rose and was quickly out of sight. The observation lasted about fifteen minutes.[7]

The foregoing could be described as archetypal – there are dozens like it in the files. The following case, by contrast, is most exceptional:

Case 62   *Serra de Almos, Spain*   *16.8.1968*

A poultry farmer saw a light like the reflection from car headlamps, while feeding his fowls around 6 am. He found a hemispherical object hovering about a metre above the ground, giving off an intense light. Two 'octopus-like' creatures, about one metre tall, with four or five legs apiece, very light in colour and thoroughly disgusting in appearance, ran to the far side of the object when he approached, and the UFO at once took off.[7]

Those who object that most reported UFO-occupants are too human in appearance could derive comfort from the foregoing case: others might attribute it to the imagination of the witness. The question of reality, which brings us close to the phenomenon of apparitions, arises in such cases as the following:

Case 63   *Aznacalzar, Spain*   *circa 5.4.1935*

Long before the UFO era, Senor Mora, a farmer, saw a large round shining object descend from the sky between 400 and 500 metres distant, at about 7.30 pm. It hovered just above the ground, and some small strange beings emerged who circled round the object. The witness thought he had experienced some kind of supernatural vision, a favour from God, and it was a central feature of his conversation until his death.[119]

Case 64   *Pontejos, Spain*   *6.1.1969*

Four people in the kitchen of a small cafe at night saw, about thirty metres distant in a nearby field, an object hovering over the ground. It appeared as an orange rectangle, about five metres long, in which the figures of five men were silhouetted. They appeared to come into the lighted area from the sides and moved towards the centre where they vanished. Then the main illumination went out, enabling the witnesses to see a large grey object, like a bowl inverted on a plate. They watched it leave, with a bright light that illuminated the neighbourhood as it went.[119]

By one of those seemingly meaningless synchronicities that bedevil ufology, an almost identical case occurred, also in Spain, at Seville nine days later: it is extremely improbable that the witness of the second case knew of the first. On both occasions one has the impression of a 'display' deliberately staged: but it does not seem likely that a spacecraft would travel across untold interstellar distances in order to perform a meaningless ballet for a few minutes in front of an audience of four kitchen workers who happen to look up from their tasks.

Such cases take us to the heart of the UFO problem: what is their purpose? But in asking such a question, we are moving from observation to interpretation, with all the risks that entails. However, even reporting an observation involves a degree of interpretation. A witness will describe a disc as 'hovering', for example, because that is what it looks as though it is doing; but this may not be an accurate description – it might really be 'resting' on a cushion created by a force field. Clearly we must be careful not to impose our own logic on their activities.

But what conceivable logic can there be for the UFOs' behaviour? Our earthly aircraft fly from A to B because its passengers want to be at B rather than A: UFOs seem to dart about the sky pointlessly, coming from nowhere, going nowhere, and doing damn all in the meantime.

When our astronauts land on the moon, they at once embark on a highly efficient programme of tasks: the only UFO occupants who seem to have any purpose in life are the dubious types who bring us all-too-human messages, and choose people like Adamski and George King as interplanetary ambassadors.

Other suggestions have been offered. Perhaps they crave some mineral that our planet possesses but theirs lacks. Perhaps they are surveying our planet as the prelude to invasion or conquest. Dramatic scenarios have been proposed in which the UFOs contain emissaries of a dying planet searching for a new home: this was the theme of a recent alleged abduction case, *The Janos People*, the pathetic tale of a kindly people who seek only living space on Earth where they can start life anew... [82] Unfortunately, even if true, such stories cannot account for the entire UFO phenomenon.

In the abduction of witnesses for the purpose of medical examination we might seem to have a recurrent behaviour pattern that conforms to human logic: which is why the story of Barney and Betty Hill (Case 17) has received so sympathetic a hearing. But a dispassionate evaluation of these events shows that the inspections themselves are perfunctory and superficial, and beset with features that often seem to relate to the individual psychology of the individual witness.

It seems not only unflattering but also illogical that they should display such concern for us as a species, while taking no interest whatever in what – as a species – we have accomplished. It would appear that no UFO has ever displayed any curiosity about our achievements – our cities, our artistic monuments and so on: just occasionally they seem to display a flicker of interest in our power supply, our atomic installations and suchlike technological advances. All of which implies a sadly materialistic attitude of mind: it could well be that when we make contact at last, we shall find the UFO people an uncultivated and boorish lot with very limited conversation.

*   *   *   *

Even if we make every conceivable allowance, the evidence derived from what witnesses report gives no satisfactory explanation of the motivation and purpose of the UFOs, nor is it compatible with any idea of motivation or purpose that any theorist has been able to devise, however freely he allows his imagination to wander. We do have some instances in which individual UFOs seem to display purposeful activity – surveillance of an aircraft, pursuing a car or a train, taking samples of lavender bushes, medical examination of humans – but none of these even begins to offer a rationale for the phenomenon as a whole. Which leaves us with a choice of very unpalatable options:

* Those who control the UFOs, for all their technological brilliance, are stupid in other respects. Possibly their biological make-up is such as to give them all the know-how needed for space travel, but none for any other activities, just as some species on earth are unbeatable at building nests but cannot for the life of them compose a string quartet.

* Their purposes may be so obscure as to be beyond our comprehension, making sense only on a cosmic level for which we are not equipped.

* What is reported is not what it seems to be. The reality is a conspiracy on a colossal scale by forces unknown, or a highly sophisticated experiment by superhuman scientists studying us as we study fruitfly or rats.

* Witnesses are not really perceiving what they think they are perceiving. The UFO phenomenon is a highly sophisticated kind of hallucination, operating on a global scale but with individual differentiation.

SIX: THE SCEPTIC'S VIEW

The evidence for UFOs is so ambiguous, contradictory and illogical that it is hardly surprising that many regard it as proof of human fallibility and gullibility, rather than evidence for a new and scientifically important phenomenon. What is more surprising is the number who, after the briefest acquaintance with the evidence, refuse to examine it further on the grounds that since such things *cannot* happen, they *did not* happen.

An unfortunate consequence has been that scientific study of the phenomenon has been inhibited. True, UFOs have been studied more fully than perhaps any other anomalous phenomenon: an indication is given by Lind's catalog of UFO journals, which requires 281 pages simply to list those in the English language.[96] But while this represents a great deal of dedicated investigation, it is no substitute for organized scientific research.

The one major venture in this category was sadly bungled. In 1966 the United States Air Force, under considerable public pressure to settle the UFO problem one way or the other, invited a number of American universities to undertake a comprehensive survey. Such was the low prestige of the subject at the time, thanks to its sensationalized popular image, that most of those who were invited turned the offer down, fearing to make themselves ridiculous by accepting . Eventually the University of Colorado accepted the offer, and the inquiry, to be led by the eminent physicist Dr Edward U. Condon, received an initial contract for a fifteen-month survey on a budget of $313,000, subsequently increased to twenty-four months and $525,000.

Almost from the start the project was bedevilled by internal disagreements. Accusations have been made that the committee was under instructions to come up with a negative conclusion: this is probably an exaggeration, but there is no doubt that some of its leading members adopted a negative attitude from the start, for one of them, project co-ordinator Robert Low, was unwise enough to commit some of his ideas to a written memorandum which was discovered and published, leading to the resignation of some of the team. Dr Condon himself behaved in an extraordinary manner, publicly airing his negative views and ridiculing the subject.

When the committee's report was eventually published in 1968, in three massive volumes totalling 1465 pages, it opened, strangely enough, with Condon's conclusions and recommendations, which were predictably negative:

Our general conclusion is that nothing has come from the study of UFOs in the past 21 years that has added to scientific knowledge. Careful consideration of the record as it is available to us leads us to conclude that further extensive study of UFOs probably cannot be justified in the expectation that science will be advanced thereby.[37]

As one critic observed, Condon might have come to a different conclusion if he had read his own report. Though ill-balanced and ill-considered, it is none the less one of the most important books on the subject ever published, and contains a mass of significant material, which not only gives the lie to the project leader's conclusions, but offers a basis for a rich research programme. This is true even of Dr Condon's own contributions, which, while inevitably reflecting his own prejudices, are nonetheless intelligent and perceptive. The sad thing is that this report, had it been more flexibly planned and more open-minded in its approach, could indeed have been the basis for 'the scientific study of UFOs' that its title claims.

Instead, what happened was that the heavily negative

conclusion, placed at the outset of this report, discouraged most readers from studying the remainder too closely: only a few persisted long enough to discover that, even among the sparse and unrepresentative selection of cases selected by the Committee, there was fully sufficient to constitute impressive evidence (among them were our Cases 22, 26, 58 and 59).

Like any other field of study, ufology can only benefit from a sympathetic scepticism, if only as a corrective to the emotional adoption of a predetermined position which, as we have already noted, often leads to uncritical acceptance of witness claims. Writers like astronomer Donald Menzel and aviation journalist Philip Klass have often done a salutary job in debunking the UFO record of some of its rubbishy cases. They would have done better still if they had not continually overstated their case. Klass, in his first book,[91] sought to show that all UFOs were freak atmospheric electrical phenomena, created by nature under rare conditions; his theory was patently inadequate to account for more than a small share, if any, of the evidence. In his second book he was more restrained, and its publisher claimed that he 'carefully and scientifically analyzes the full spectrum of the UFO question'.[92] In fact, he does nothing of the kind; he selects certain cases and shows the investigation or the analysis to have been at fault. Much of this is first-rate, and would be welcomed by any serious ufologist.

It is not easy to illustrate the attitude and methods of such writers, because in order to appreciate them a detailed study of the case is required. However, this case illustrates the sceptical method at its crudest:

Case 65   *Near Norfolk, Virginia, USA*   *14.7.1952*

A Pan American DC4, piloted by Captain Nash and Second Officer Fortenberry, was approaching Norfolk at about 8.10 pm when both men noticed a red brilliance in the sky, which quickly resolved itself into six bright objects, fiery red in appearance, streaking towards their aircraft. Their shape was clearly outlined, not fuzzy, as flat discs about thirty metres in diameter, and very thin, no more than five metres thick. The DC4 was flying at 2500 metres, and they estimated the objects, flying below them, as being at about 600 metres. They were in tightly stepped formation, but when they were almost directly beneath the aircraft they flipped up on edge simultaneously and made a 150-degree turn; at this point they were joined by two others. The lights suddenly blinked out, then came back on again; the objects sped away in an arc which took them above the altitude of the DC4. Then the lights went out one after the other in sequence. The entire observation lasted about fifteen seconds. In computing the speed of the objects, the witnesses tried to be conservative, but insisted that it could not have been much under 20,000 km/h[116]

Physicist Charles Maney challenged Professor Menzel to account for this circumstantial and detailed sighting. Menzel responded to the challenge, explaining his reasons thus: 'Some day, the historian will want to know the facts underlying the UFO hysteria of the last decade or so . . . My rather voluminous correspondence with Maney was interesting because it helped clarify my picture of a man with a scientific background who still believed in the reality of the UFO.'[53]

The reader may also feel it helps clarify our picture of a man who was determined *not* to believe in the reality of the UFO. At various stages in that voluminous correspondence, Menzel offered the following explanations for the two pilots' sighting:

1. Autokinesis (subjective shifts of judgement).

2. Reflection in the window of the plane.

3. The hostess taking a drag on a cigarette.

4. Reflection from a swinging door opening into the cabin.

5. A sharply focussed searchlight shining through layers of air caused by temperature inversion.

The impression we get is that Menzel was willing to entertain any conjecture, no matter how implausible, rather than admit that the two men may have actually seen what they claimed to see. No serious ufologist would argue against making every effort to find a natural explanation if it meets the case, but here Menzel is ignoring the greater part of the testimony in order to fit the sighting to his current explanation.

In other instances, where the evidence is too explicit to be set aside, the sceptics have recourse to a multiple solution to what seems a single problem. When a pilot named Gorman was about to land his light plane at night, he was 'buzzed' by a rapidly manoeuvring ball of light, which could also be seen from the control tower. Professor Menzel's proposal was that Gorman was seeing a lighted balloon some of the time, and a mirage of the planet Jupiter the rest of the time.[104] To mistake one natural object for a UFO could happen to anyone; but to mistake two, on a single occasion, strains credibility more than the possibility that Gorman was really confronted by an unknown object.

Sceptics of the generation of Condon, Menzel and Klass seem to have come to the UFO problem determined not to accept *any* of the evidence but to accept *any* alternative, however improbable. A more open-minded approach is represented by Michel Monnerie, an experienced French investigator who shook his colleagues in 1977 when he published a book titled *Et si les OVNIs n'existent pas? ('And suppose the UFOs don't exist?')*[110] Monnerie, on the basis of cases he had personally researched, decided that the level of distortion and invention was so high as to justify the conclusion that all UFO sightings could be dismissed on similar grounds. Here is one of his instances:

Case 66   *Lot, France*   7.5.1972

A lady went out onto her balcony to close the blinds and had a feeling as though she was being watched. Lifting her head, she saw a light, which she at first took for an enormous star; but it was more like a fireball, emitting colours – orange, green, red, pink. Sometimes it seemed to shrink, sometimes to swell. All her family came out to see it. The following evening it returned, and she saw it descend, then stop; make an abrupt movement, then stop again. There were similar performances on subsequent evenings: one night it was so bright as to light up the entire balcony. Yet investigation showed that the planet Venus was in that sector of the sky on those evenings, and this was almost certainly what the witness had seen.

Monnerie's thesis for such cases is that a banal observation of an aeroplane, or the planet Venus, or whatever, triggers a 'waking dream', in which the subconscious mind takes over and replaces what is really there with a dream-fiction which the witness sincerely believes he is seeing.

That such psychological processes can and do occur is beyond question, and many ufologists would agree that this is a viable explanation for many dubious cases, particularly where there are personal factors involved, as in the following case:

Case 67   *Australia*   *no date; late 1970s?*

'Mr A.' felt a strong impulse to go to the local airport; there he saw a bright round light in the sky which he reported as a UFO. Investigation showed the witness to be a 58-year-old immigrant, recently arrived in Australia, living alone, with a history of trouble at work, a sense of persecution, and many other stories of anomalous experiences.[112]

In such a case it is surely correct of Mark Moravec, who investigated the case, to conclude that 'Mr A. has merely incorporated UFO material into his delusions.' Some such process as Monnerie proposes may well be involved. But does the same apply to, say, the Nash-Fortenberry case (Case 65)? It is surely overstretching the hypothesis to apply it as a universal explanation.

Nevertheless, informed scepticism like Monnerie's does ufology a valuable service, both as a source of potentially valid ideas and also by compelling the rest of us to maintain a critical attitude. His work demonstrates, too, that the most effective criticism of the UFO evidence has always come from within the ranks of ufologists, from those who are acquainted with the full scope of the phenomenon. When American investigator Allan Hendry published his *UFO Handbook* in 1979, he gave ufological hot-heads a much-needed douche of cold water. The major part of his book comprises a catalogue of the various ways in which witnesses have misinterpreted everyday things as UFOs:

Case 68   *California, USA*   *No date given*

A waitress, returning home about 4 am, saw an object that she estimated as being about eight metres in diameter, with red, green and blue flashing lights, and a cloudy haze surrounding it. Two other witnesses confirmed the sighting. She saw it hover stationary over a hospital for about fifty minutes, then shoot up into the sky; at the same time two smaller objects near to it, star-like but with pulsating colours, also vanished. During the observation lights in a nearby parking lot dimmed and brightened intermittently, leading the witness to conjecture that the UFO might somehow be drawing power from them. Animals were affected – a dog howled and barked, a parakeet screeched; she herself felt as though she were in a trance, drained of energy and feeling it an effort to move. Nonetheless, despite this wealth of detail, Hendry established that the witness had been contemplating nothing more exotic than the moon, with the planets Mars and Jupiter in visual proximity.[76]

Such observations demonstrate the importance of a

wide perspective. It was Hendry's knowledge of astronomy that enabled him to correct the waitress' misinterpretation, while Moravec's familiarity with psychological processes gave him confidence to question 'Mr A.'s claim. In its early days, UFO investigation was hampered by doubts as to what discipline of study was best fitted to tackle the problem – was it the astronomer, the engineer or the physicist whose expertise was most relevant? Today we would say that not only can all three contribute, but also the psychologist, the sociologist and even the mythologist.

What these specialists can do is open investigators' eyes to the range of possibilities available. French ufologist Jacques Vallée has drawn parallels between many UFO sightings and stories from folklore:[152] Belgian author Bertrand Méheust has demonstrated coincidence-defying similarities between UFO reports and certain science fiction stories.[101] But neither would make the mistake of supposing that he has a blanket explanation which will account for the entire UFO phenomenon: they have simply drawn our attention to aspects which may contribute to our understanding of the problem, even if to begin with they seem only to be complicating it.

Similarly in the field of psychology. Recently Alvin Lawson of California has proffered the thesis that abduction subjects are in fact re-living birth trauma experiences.[94] He has made a very suggestive case, but he would not for a moment suggest that he has 'explained' the UFO: he has simply proposed a 'testable hypothesis', which could lead to positive and scientifically valid conclusions.

Scepticism at this level can do nothing but good. Those who take the close-minded approach, on the contrary, starting not from the evidence but from an a priori assumption that the phenomena *cannot* exist and therefore there *must* be an alternative explanation, merely place a stumbling-block in the way of effective research. Fortunately, such an attitude is confined to a few individuals; and their failure, despite all their strident assertions, to resolve the UFO enigma, is the best possible testimonial to the strength of the evidence.

SEVEN:
ANALYSING THE EVIDENCE

Despite important and significant exceptions, it is clear that the overwhelming implication of UFO evidence points to the *apparent* existence of a diversity of structured objects, with a technical capability far exceeding anything that exists on Earth, and which is evidently under intelligent control. In addition, a substantial proportion of these objects appear to contain beings who are not like any creatures on Earth; and who seem, over and above their superior mastery of aeronautics, to be more advanced in knowledge and perhaps in wisdom also.

The inference that our Earth is being visited by beings from other worlds, in their vehicles, is hard to avoid. However, in addition to the total absence of solid evidence to this effect, and the inherent improbabilities involved, there are a number of additional factors which must be taken into account.

The psychic connection
This can take many forms: the following are the most frequent:

*Premonitions that UFO sightings will take place. Frequently this amounts to no more than an impulse to go to the window, or onto the front lawn – whereupon, lo and behold, the witness does indeed see a UFO! On occasions, though, a specific prediction is made, days or weeks in advance, that a UFO will be seen in a certain place. In 1974 the chaplain on a French air base, Père Mollison, an amateur hypnotist, reported a prediction from one of his subjects that a UFO sighting would occur three days later at a certain village. A local UFO investigative group was on hand at the predicted time and place and did indeed see five balls of blue light.[43]

* Many witnesses claim to be in telepathic contact with beings seen or unseen. M. Masse, in our Case 6, reported a sense of rapport with the entities he saw in his lavender field, but sometimes the contact is more specific. Rutledge's *Project Identification*[131] affords many instances in which the object under observation responds not only to physical events on the ground but also to mental suggestions, and I personally have met a witness who seemed able to cause UFOs to change direction in obedience to her mental wishes.

* A number of witnesses have reported poltergeist-type incidents in their homes as a consequence of, or associated with, UFO sightings. I have personally investigated two such cases, and there are many more in the records. Here, we have to ask whether the UFO sighting triggered off the rest, or should itself be regarded as one of the poltergeist phenomena.

* Many witnesses have reported 'missing time' experiences in connection with UFO sightings; this is of course a standard feature of abduction cases. I do not know of a single instance in which this feeling of a time-lapse has been objectively confirmed. Witnesses report returning home and finding that their journey has taken, let us say, two hours longer than expected, but there is never anyone sitting up waiting for them who can confirm the fact. The question also arises, where was the witness – who is often in a car – during the time-lapse? Thus the time-lapse phenomenon is linked with the 'traffic-free' phenomenon. In the 'Antonia' case, witness Hélène Giuliana claimed that in the summer of 1976 she went aboard an alien spacecraft, leaving her car, with its lights out, on the Route National 531. Investigators established

that at such a time, traffic would have been so heavy on that road that a vehicle would pass on the average every eleven seconds! Clearly, the incident could not have taken place as the witness reported it.[126]

* Some witnesses have felt impelled to practice automatic writing in connection with their sighting. Generally this is something that happens afterwards, when the incident is over, and most often the witness claims to be responding to some kind of irresistible impulse. The messages usually purport to come from the extraterrestrial entities responsible for the UFO sighting, who have used this means of establishing contact. The usual contactee-type messages then follow – establishing an identity, giving warnings and the like. A classic instance is that of Mrs Keech, whose messages led to the creation of a group who expected to be 'rescued' by extraterrestrials from an impending disaster threatening our Earth: fortunately, or otherwise, neither the rescue nor the disaster took place as predicted.[54] On the other hand Jacques Vallée tells of a Mrs Swan whose automatic writing was studied by American and Canadian authorities, and reportedly led to a dramatic sighting in 1959 by Naval Intelligence personnel, who looked out of their window as instructed and saw a disc-shaped object in the afternoon sky over Washington![153]

* A certain number of witnesses have reported apparitions in connection with their sightings. In November 1957 an entity, who claimed to be extraterrestrial and communicated with the witness telepathically, manifested – slowly – in the kitchen of Mrs Cynthia Appleton, a 27-year-old housewife from Aston, Birmingham.[22]

There are basically two ways of coming to terms with such reports. On the one hand, we may start from the assumption that UFOs are indeed extraterrestrial spacecraft, with no psychic or psychological nonsense about them; in which case, it would seem likely that most, if not all, of these alleged psychic incidents are psychological in origin.

Australian researcher Mark Moravec has shown that psychological processes exist that would account satisfactorily for these illusions being mistaken for reality.[1] If his diagnosis is correct, such cases are not strictly speaking UFO incidents at all, but psychological events personal to the witness, which happen to exploit the trappings of a UFO event because they are suitable expressions for whatever problem or preoccupation is troubling him.

On the other hand, it may indeed be that these psychic events are an inherent part of the UFO phenomenon, and that the psychic dimension is inseparable from the rest. Rutledge's findings (and they are by no means unique) strongly suggest that the UFOs, or those who control them, are able to monitor our thought processes. There is nothing necessarily supernatural about this, of course: our brains operate by means of electrical impulses, and as such are capable – in principle – of detection. Nonetheless, the implications are formidable.

It is clearly too soon to decide which of these options is correct; consequently, however distasteful we may find them, we have no right to exclude these psychic occurrences from the body of UFO evidence.

The science-fiction and folklore connections
Consider these two excerpts:

'It came along over the hill, and quick as an arrow it swooped down till I thought it would have crushed me. But all of a sudden it seemed to see this tree beneath which I'm standing, and like a dart it turns and whizzes away . . . It seemed to be alive and thinking . . . There wasn't a sound; it came swooping over the village, gave a kind of dull flash, and then was gone, melted into the night as it were. But it came again . . . and hung there, like a great square patch of cloud, without so much as a movement. Then it dropped like a stone, leaned to one side, and came swooping over my head, and . . . with a flash, it was gone.'[24]

'I saw it about seventy metres away, manoeuvring for about ninety seconds in all kinds of strange and varied positions. It moved in total silence, floating slowly at about a hundred metres altitude. Suddenly it started to drop with an oscillating movement, and I could see it turn on its side. Abruptly it shot like an arrow to one side, so fast that it vanished from my sight, only to surprise me be reappearing lower down, where it came to a sudden stop, swinging from one side to the other. For about four seconds it hung completely motionless in the air, silent but with a slight vibration. Then suddenly it shuddered two or three times, made a right angle turn and disappeared like a flash.'[101]

The similarity between the two passages is certainly striking, though the second is an Argentinian UFO sighting of the 1970s while the first is an excerpt from an English adventure story of 1911. One or two such parallels might be regarded as coincidence, but Belgian author Bertrand Méheust has filled a whole book with them,[101] and there does seem to be more than coincidence involved. However, it is a challenge to conjecture how such a correspondence can be accounted for: illiterate Argentinian peasants are unlikely to be familiar with English adventure-stories of seventy years ago. Some fairly exotic scenarios have been proposed,[49] usually implying some kind of 'image bank', wherefrom all parties derive their material; such processes necessarily imply that the UFO experience is fundamentally a subjective one, though this does not necessarily imply that it has no real dimension to it.

Similar complexities arise from similarities between UFO experiences and folklore stories. Abductions by fairies have much in common with abductions by extra-terrestrial aliens, as Vallée has demonstrated.[152] And French researcher Jean Bastide is only one of many who have hunted through ancient chronicles and shown how, with a little goodwill, many incidents, both in history and fable, in biblical records and in the oral traditions of primitive societies, could be interpreted as UFO events.[9] Though the resemblances are often strained by ufologists eager to establish a long if not honourable ancestry for

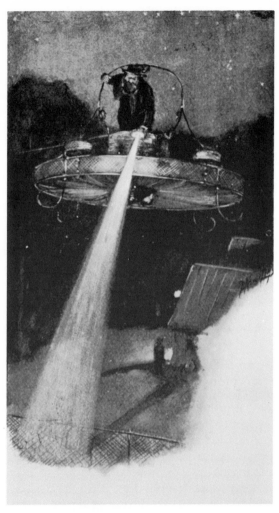

Fiction anticipates fact. Illustration to Frank Stockton's story *The Great Stone of Sardis*, in *Harper's Monthly*, New York, 1897. This compares quite closely with such sightings as that of Cowichan (Case 5), the biggest difference being that the early flying object has no transparent dome. The beam of light, not reported from Cowichan, is virtually a standard feature in a high proportion of UFO reports, and the object is shown hovering over a house at night in a manner which is very commonly claimed.

their subject, there are a sufficient number of convincing instances to prevent us dismissing such evidence entirely.

The BVM Connection
Independent research in both France and Italy has established beyond question that a statistical link exists between UFO sightings on the one hand, and visions of the Blessed Virgin Mary on the other.[97, 147] French researcher Gilbert Cornu has shown how, in 1947, the year when Kenneth Arnold's headlined sighting made the world aware of flying saucers, there was a very sharp increase in the number of reports of visions of the Virgin: another exceptional upsurge occurred in 1954, when there was also a dramatic UFO wave in France and Spain.

The correspondence is far too pronounced to be ascribed to coincidence. But what does it imply? We have three basic options:

* The Virgin Mary is responsible for UFO sightings.

* UFOs include phenomena which may be mistaken for the Virgin Mary.

* One and the same state of affairs is responsible for causing some people to see the Virgin Mary, others to see UFOs.

Elaborations are also conceivable. A theorist who believed UFOs to be instruments of Satan might propose that the Virgin makes additional appearances whenever UFOs manifest in exceptional numbers, to counter the diabolical influence and comfort her admirers. However one interprets it, the correlation is a significant item of evidence which must be taken into account.

The geophysical connection
Those who study 'earth mysteries' have long maintained that there is a link between UFOs and geophysical phenomena, and French ufologist Fernand Lagarde has supported this view by his analysis of French sightings.[97]

This has led to a number of theories ranging from the down-to-earth to the unashamedly occult: options include the following:

* UFOs are a physical product of earth forces, ball-lightning-like plasma, perhaps, produced by piezo-electric effects and escaping into the atmosphere.

* UFOs, from sources unknown, are attracted to, interested in, or have affinity for places where earth forces manifest, such as geological faults.

* Earth forces generate a state of mind in the witness that is either favourable to or actually induces the sighting of UFOs.

Until more data is available, such an approach can only be speculative: but there are theorists who believe it is here that the key to the UFO enigma will be found.

The space age connection
An aspect of the UFO phenomenon which is so obvious that it is easily overlooked is the correlation with our own first tentative probing into space. This correlation can be used to support either the extraterrestrial or the socio-logical approach. On the one hand, it is suggested that the inhabitants of other worlds, observing that humankind is just about to join 'the galactic club', are naturally concerned to make sure we are eligible as members, and are checking up on us accordingly.

Those who incline to believe that the UFOs are some-how products of psychological processes will see the space age connection quite differently. We are all space conscious today, as witness the films we see, the books we read, even the advertising in our press and television. Consequently, the 'myth' of alien visitors, exploring us as we plan to explore them, is a powerful emotional source of imagery and symbol, onto which we can tag our hopes and fears, our guilt and our dreams. Linking up with the 'folklore connection', this approach interprets the UFO simply as the space-age version of a perennial phenomenon: other ages had religious myths, demons, witches, fairies and so forth; we have the UFO and the alien visitor.

In addition to these general parameters, there are a number of minor anomalies related to the UFO phenomenon, some of which we have already noted. Many of these may turn out to be only secondary or even totally irrelevant; but until we know for sure, we cannot leave them out of our analysis.

* The number of *'repeater cases'*, involving a witness who sees UFOs on several separate occasions, seems to defy statistics. Does this mean that certain people, or certain types of people, are 'favoured' by UFOs? Or does it indicate that UFOs are a product of the witness' mind?

* There seems to be *'window' areas*, where UFOs manifest more frequently than elsewhere. Is this fact or illusion; if fact, is it geological, topographical or sociological?

* UFOs seem to manifest in waves or *'flaps'*. Again, is this a real or a social phenomenon?

* UFO experiences in some countries differ in kind from those elsewhere. Thus French catalogues indicate a far higher proportion of landing cases than the United States, while the Latin Americans seem to be plagued by hostile and aggressive visitors.

* Is the failure to produce convincing photographic evidence a technical or a psychological problem? Is the alleged 'vanishing' of so many original negatives and documents a real phenomenon or a symptom of the paranoia that underlies the entire UFO question?

* UFO sightings seem to follow a line of development towards ever greater sophistication and credibility. Even leaving aside the 1896 airships and the 1946 ghost

rockets, we have seen UFOs develop from distantly-glimpsed discs to closely-encountered objects observed in detail (compare our Case 55 – the original Arnold sighting – with Case 23 – the Cash/Landrum experience). Similarly, unbelievable 'contacts' have been superceded by plausible 'abductions'. Does this represent a real development on the part of those who are responsible for the UFOs, or should it be seen as the natural escalation of a myth?

*The UFO phenomenon, as such, is associated with a number of other anomalies. The most dramatic of these is the 'Men in Black' scenario. Typically, a trio of well-dressed men, uncannily like the popular image of American secret service agents, turn up on the doorstep of UFO witnesses, claiming an authority that is later shown to be spurious. They frequently behave in a way which suggests they are not human, and utter threats which prove to be without force. It is easy to interpret them as folklore figures – there is nothing new about men dressed in black in the annals of legend: but if so, does it follow that the UFOs to which they relate are equally mythical, or are they mythical parasites battening on a genuine phenomenon?

We may ask the same question about some other anomalies. Is it paranoia, again, that links UFOs with the baffling matter of cattle mutilation across many of the United States? Colorado author Frederick Smith[136] concluded that the two problems are intimately linked: 'From the UFO buff's point of view the cattle mutilation phenomenon provides some remarkable new facts and problems, things we should have been thinking about but preferred not to.' Another bizarre connection is with 'Bigfoot', the extraordinary humanoid creature who seems to exist on the fringe of reality – and who is seen too often in connection with UFOs for the connection to be in doubt.[33] But *what* connection? Does Bigfoot come from the UFOs? Or are the UFOs interested in Bigfoot?

Or are both UFOs and Bigfoot products of some deeper process? Yet again, there is a wealth of options: but the connection is beyond question, just as it is with 'moth-man', another 'creature of the outer edge' whose existence has yet to be established, but has frequently been reported in circumstances that indicate a link with the UFO phenomenon.[86]

*   *   *   *

One way or another, all the connections outlined in the foregoing pages have to be taken into account when we analyze the UFO evidence. It is tempting to favour the psychological/sociological approach, because this offers a way of evading the factual side of the issue. Reports of many if not all of the phenomena can be ascribed to paranoia, or social anxiety, the trauma induced by the nuclear age and so on, and that way the problem gets to be a lot simpler. But while the psychologist undoubtedly has some of the answers, he has yet to convince us that he has them all: it would be premature to accept his offer to let us off the hook.

In the pages that follow, then, we are concerned with the *whole* phenomenon, in all its baffling complexity, with all its ambiguities and absurdities, its inconsistencies and paradoxes. We shall assume that the evidence presented earlier in this book can be accepted as a more or less accurate account of what the witness observed. While accepting that hoaxers and liars may be responsible for a small part, and while accepting that if we had more data we might be able to find natural explanations for some others, we shall assume that the evidence as we possess it gives us a fair approximation to an accurate description.

Most explanations are variations on one of five basic hypotheses, that UFOs are:

* natural phenomena;
* artefacts of terrestrial origin;
* artefacts of extraterrestrial origin;

* psychological manifestations; or
* cultural manifestations

Let us now see how our evidence matches up with each of these in turn.

UFOs as natural phenomena

A very great many UFO sightings are misinterpretations of natural phenomena, more or less familiar. The question remains, whether some of them may be natural phenomena at present unknown to science.

Explanations along these lines fall into two categories, the biological and the meteorological. The most specific claims in the former category are those of Trevor James Constable (Case 43), who produced photographs of jellyfish-like objects in the atmosphere which he recorded on infra-red film. Unfortunately there has been no substantial confirmation of his work, nor any evidence to support it from other sources.

The case for a meteorological explanation is much stronger. The variously named 'ghost lights' reported in specific locations throughout the world, sometimes over a very long period, are an obvious candidate. Consider this case:

Case 69   Brown Mountain, North Carolina, USA   reported 1951

A local filling station proprietor, one of many investigators who have sought to explain the famous 'Brown Mountain Lights', went onto the mountain one night with a group of friends. After spending several fruitless hours, they were preparing to leave when a strong light, as long as his outstretched arm, formed a few metres above the heads of the party. It hovered motionless for a while, emitting a sizzling sound: then it began to pulsate, growing alternately longer and shorter in length, before finally vanishing.[15]

The fact that such lights have been reported in some cases as occurring for more than a hundred years encourages us to look for a purely geophysical explanation: at the same time, the object seems to have displayed at least a degree of intelligent control in manifesting over the heads of the investigators, unless, of course, we presume that the body-warmth or some other physical properties of the humans attracted the phenomenon automatically. This would hardly account, however, for cases which appear quite similar, such as the Hebron police encounter (Case 41), where the light was seen in the same location on several occasions.

Ball lightning is frequently proposed as an explanation,[91] but the performance of UFOs quite transcends anything reported of ball lightning[8, 46] and we would have to presume a highly developed form to account for the observations. Considering that ball lightning itself is so rare a phenomenon that its existence was until recently doubted even by scientists working in the meteorological field, to propose the existence of an even more rarefied variant of it to account for the entire UFO phenomenon with its tens of thousands of sightings is hardly logical.

The evidence of Rutledge and his team, noted in Chapter One, is probably the most substantial indication that there exist, within our atmosphere, intelligent ball-of-light objects which seem to lack any 'space-ship' attributes. Could such a phenomenon be involved in the following case?

Case 70   Near Washington, DC, USA   'recent' in 1976

The witnesses, one of them a technically experienced civilian employee at a military installation, reported seeing two anomalous objects in the midday sky. They were bright, apparently luminous, and circular: they were seen in a cloudless sky with visibility about 30 kilometres. No aircraft, balloons, etc., were to be seen. The objects descended 'from the blue' one after the other and remained at a certain point for a minute or more. The witnesses noted faint dark rings about the central bright sections of the objects. After a while the second appearing object executed a left-right zigzag movement, then rose rapidly up; moments later the other object also began a rapid vertical ascent. Both vanished out of sight.[39]

As the reporter of this case, himself a research physicist for the United States government, comments, 'It is difficult to decide what to make of a report like this.' It could with some show of reason be related to either a natural or a man-made object, and if no other kind of UFO were ever reported, it would be the more economical choice, scientifically speaking, to decide in favour of a natural phenomenon, albeit of an unknown kind.

But of course by far the greatest number of UFO sightings, in which the object is described in any useful detail, clearly indicate a structured object which would seem to be an artefact. If accurately reported, they would seem to refute explanation in terms of a natural phenomenon for all but a minority of sightings.

However, earth forces researcher Paul Devereux has proposed a possible way of reconciling the natural-origin hypothesis with the *un*natural appearance of so many UFOs.[44] He postulates that UFOs are 'non-sentient, geophysically produced phenomena – transient pockets of energy or tenuous matter – produced anywhere under the right conditions but particularly in areas of geological faulting or disturbance', and goes on to suggest that 'the terrestrial discharge phenomenon seems able, under certain circumstances that are by no means clear, to act as a carrier of imagery, its own substance accommodating the image's form'. The imagery, that is, derives from human consciousness – the mind of the witness: the UFOs adopt the appropriate form by modifying their own substance. This is not far removed from the old Theosophists' account of fairies which, they say, are fundamentally amorphous creatures with no determined appearance, who take on a specific 'fairy-like' form which they know, by reading the witness's mind, he expects to see.[63]

By bringing the witness into the business as an active

contributor, so to speak, such a hypothesis not only answers the awkward question, how do shapeless natural objects come to be mistaken for clearly structured objects, but also explains why so many witnesses see so many different types of UFO. But in answering these questions it leaves many others unanswered. It does not, for instance, explain why some of us 'expect' to see alien spaceships disgorging beautiful spacepersons, while others get to see boring nothings in the sky, as in Case 70 above. Consider the following case:

Case 71   *Dax, France*   *4.6.1968*

A young French couple, M. and Mme Grammont, were driving at night along a Route Nationale, when they suddenly saw before them, about a hundred metres ahead on the traffic-free road, a dark hemispherical mass, as wide as the road and about three metres high, seemingly resting on the road and with a red winking light on top of the dome. Although it looked soft and vaporous, the driver thought there must have been some kind of accident, and slammed on his brakes. The engine cut out just before reaching the object, but the vehicle slid on, still travelling at a fair speed. To their amazement they felt nothing, but just went straight into the object which disappeared from sight as they 'hit' it. There was no impact, no heat, no sound, no discomfort of any kind. They paused a moment, then drove on.[97]

Here indeed is a case which, on the face of it, could be explained as a geopsychic incident, in which a geophysical emanation was really and truly sitting there in the driver's path, and simultaneously modified its appearance so that both simultaneously saw an identical UFO-like object. But the geopsychic explanation is just one of several possible explanations, ranging from the meteorological to the psychological. Tempting as it is to espouse a hypothesis that offers to account for so much, we must face the fact that it involves a deal of speculation without a scrap of positive evidence. This being so, we are bound to consider the alternatives.

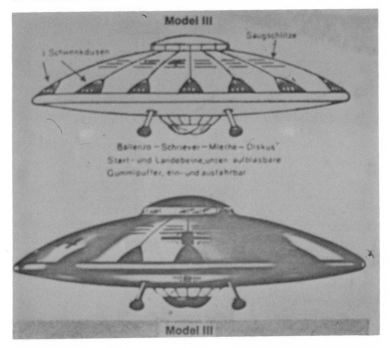

German disc project of *circa* 1944. It is claimed that this object, or a variant of it, actually flew successfully; it attained very high speeds compared to aircraft of the day, but was very difficult to control. From Mattern, *UFO's Unbekanntes Flugobjekt,* Ontario, Canada.

UFOs as artefacts of terrestrial origin

In the first years of the current UFO era, shortly after the end of World War Two, it was perhaps a natural assumption that the flying saucers were secret devices of rival military powers. At the termination of hostilities both Russia and America gained access to information about advanced research being conducted by German scientists, and were able to abduct some of the scientists themselves into the bargain. A veritable mystique has grown up about the results of this research, and perhaps the Nazi inventors gained more than their fair share of kudos because their work was revealed to the world while the victorious powers naturally kept quiet about whatever secret projects they had in hand. Even so, the solid achievement of the V1 and V2 rockets is painful evidence of their very real skill.

Among the Nazi projects was a disc-shaped aircraft, which is supposed to have performed very impressively in test flights. This had led some theorists to suppose that UFOs are lineal descendents of Nazi weapons.[155] Others went further still, telling how the Nazis had prepared secret bases in the antarctic even before the war, and that at the end of the war in Europe Hitler was taken by U-boat to one such base, where Nazi colonies were established, and where the disc aircraft were developed to become the UFOs of today, operating peacefully as had always been Hitler's intention, had he not been misunderstood by his scheming enemies.[100]

While few were prepared to swallow the Antarctic hypothesis, the 'made-in-Russia' explanation seemed at first to be plausible enough. During the early years of the Cold War, America's paranoid fears of Communist aggression took many bizarre forms, and in that climate it was easy to believe that UFOs were a tangible proof of the Red Menace. Loren Gross's brilliant history of the UFO phenomenon[69] reveals how one much-debated question of the 1947-8 period was whether the FBI and other security forces should involve themselves with flying saucers. When one witness reported sighting a disc in the fall of 1948 he was subjected to a security check by the OSI (Office of Special Investigations, the military's own investigative outfit): not only did they interview the witness himself, but they questioned his workmates and acquaintances about his character, his integrity and, of course, his loyalty, as though seeing a UFO could somehow be construed as an un-American activity.

In time, of course, it became apparent that no other earthly power could be responsible for the UFOs. Curiously, though, the Antarctic hypothesis has been revived, though in a different form. More than one contactee account (for instance [11]) has referred to extra-terrestrial UFO bases in the Antarctic, as well as off the Latin American coast and – inevitably – in 'the Bermuda Triangle'.[121] Other suggested locations for bases have been Corsica[32] and Stack Rock off the Welsh coast.[117]

But terrestrial hypotheses have one great advantage: they do not necessarily involve extraterrestrial visitors. One school of thought suggests that UFOs come from the Himalayas, for example, a traditional source of esoteric knowledge much valued by those who decry the materialism of the West.[56] But this very fact constitutes an objection: for while Western materialism has led to computers, *Concorde* and the digital watch, oriental wisdom tends to go in more for gurus and meditation, which does not seem consistent with high-tech developments such as the UFO.

Perhaps for this reason, other champions of a terrestrial origin have refurbished the ancient myth of the Hollow Earth and credited the UFOs to a subterranean civilization. It is conjectured that they come out through holes at the Poles.[14, 99, 145]

The concept of a less exotic terrestrial origin has never been wholly abandoned, however. The extraterrestrial hypothesis, when first formulated, swept all others before it; but of late the more mundane explanation has enjoyed something of a comeback, thanks particularly to incidents such as the Cash/Landrum case (Case 23). The 'secret project' theory has gained additional force from revelations obtained under the Freedom of Information Act in the United States, which confirm what many ufologists have long suspected. After being stigmatized for decades as a symptom of paranoia, the 'conspiracy' theory is now seen to contain a substantial portion of truth: the American government stands convicted by its own documents of lying to the public about the degree of its interest in UFOs. Watergate and other government scandals have not enhanced the credibility of the authorities, and the fact that a number of documents are still being withheld from public inspection on grounds of national security lends support to allegations of a continued cover-up.

Possibly linked to these matters are researches into supposed 'crashed saucer' incidents. Veteran UFO investigator Leonard Stringfield is in the process of gathering material that convincingly attests to a number of events, involving crashes and/or landings of airborne objects, which the United States authorities went to great lengths to conceal at the time and which remain unexplained even though some of them occurred more than thirty years ago. While most researchers believe these incidents to relate to extraterrestrial objects, they could equally well relate to, say, secret government projects. But why need the United States government go on being secretive about, say, a missile which went astray in the New Mexico desert in the 1940s?[13, 143]

What kind of fire there may be behind all this smoke remains to be shown, but beyond doubt there is something curious going on. A recent event in Russia amusingly demonstrates the misconceptions that may arise when ufology conflicts with political expediency:

Case 72   *Petrozavodsk, Russia*   *20.9.1977*

Many residents saw 'a giant glowing jellyfish UFO' hovering over the city, causing a widespread emotional response among observers. Seen from a great distance, it moved slowly to a position overhead where it hovered, showering the city with fine rays which looked like rain: then the object took on the shape of a bright semicircle, and then that of a pool of light, red in the centre and white around. In this form it moved on, and finally vanished after ten to twenty minutes of observation. Stories were told of how the rays had drilled holes in sidewalks and windows: a doctor reported how an ambulance had gone out of control due to electromagnetic effects; many feared the city was under nuclear attack.

The Russian authorities made no official pronouncement on the object, and their silence was widely taken as tacit approval of the popular belief that a UFO was responsible. Investigative groups in America, however, suspected a more mundane explanation, and without too much difficulty identified it as a secret satellite launch from Plesetsk. The Russian authorities, though officially denying the existence of UFOs, ironically found themselves having to seem to acknowledge them as a possible explanation, rather than release classified information about their space activities.[115]

Satellites and missiles have always been on any investigator's short-list of explanations. The Petrozavodsk UFO was no more than a luminous shape in the sky; at no point did any serious ufologist suppose it to be an alien spacecraft. The Cash/Landrum incident (Case 23) is another matter: could the US government be allowing the public to regard it as a UFO rather than reveal that it is experimenting with such alarming devices? And was something of the sort happening in the Farlow incident (Case 32) when the British Ministry of Defence was certainly involved, but no public statement was ever issued?

On the other hand, how long can such objects be concealed before an unmuzzled journalist sees one landing or taking off, or an incident occurs that *cannot* be explained away? The hypothesis of a terrestrial origin for UFOs makes heavy demands on our credulity. We have to suppose that there exists, somewhere on our much-travelled Earth, a nation capable of extraordinary technical development, with all that this requires in the way of plant, raw materials, deployment of workers and so forth; that it can build, house and operate flying machines often of enormous size without once revealing their place of origin; and that it is willing to fly these machines around in the sky, year after year, without making contact, peaceful or military, with other nations, and only rarely with isolated individuals; that it refrains from exercising the strategic power which such superior technology puts in its hands, and yet employs them for no other apparent purpose.

In all these respects, the supposed nation would be behaving in a manner strangely at variance with that normally associated with a human society. It is pleasant to think that in Antarctica, or the Himalayas, or the Inner Earth, there has developed a civilization superior to us not only in technology but also in wisdom. But the odds in favour of such a space-age Shangri-La remain, alas, as remote as the place itself.

UFOs as artefacts of extraterrestrial origin
The hypothesis that UFOs are the incoming equivalent of our outgoing spacecraft is far and away the most widespread and popular explanation. It seems logical that the peoples of other worlds should be as interested in visiting us as we are in visiting them. It is understandable that our own emergence into the era of nuclear power and space travel should be of interest to other peoples: indeed, until the comparatively recent technology explosion, they may not have been aware of our existence, for only with radio and other forms of radiation are we generating signs of life capable of being detected at sufficient distance. Even if they did know or suspect our existence earlier, they may have held back from contact while we were in a relatively primitive state, but now be interested in assessing our eligibility for membership of the 'galactic club'.

All these are sound, logical arguments: but they are also very human arguments. They presuppose that an alien civilization would argue along much the same lines as we do. Such may indeed be the case, but we have no right to assume it. Indeed, any similarity between them and us, physically, mentally or psychologically, may be more than we have a right to expect and certainly more than we have the right to take for granted. So it must be with the most open of minds that we assess the evidence for the extraterrestrial hypothesis.

The majority of UFOs, insofar as they are capable of being described at all, are described as structured objects with a specific shape and design features. That is to say, they look as if someone made them: and if, as we have seen, it is unlikely that they were made by anyone here on Earth, then it follows they were made by someone somewhere else in Space.

Unfortunately, the simple logic of this reasoning has to face some substantial objections, as regards the objects themselves, what they do, where they come from, and when they have elected to show themselves. Let us consider these four points in turn.

*UFOs could conceivably be spacecraft. They are not very like our own spacecraft, but we should not expect them to be: and some of them make good sense even in terms of terrestrial engineering. (Several engineers have had fun conjecturing about the technology of UFOs, based on witness reports. See, for instance, [23, 40, 118, 160].) What is more disconcerting is the great variety of shapes and sizes. An analogy has been drawn with the diversity of motor car models on our planet: but is it legitimate to think that interplanetary spacecraft would be as subject to taste and whim as personal surface transportation?

Ufologists have interpreted this diversity in differing ways. American researcher Wendelle Stevens, who has a massive collection of alleged UFO photos, states that 'in all these thousand-odd cases, there are less than five where two different reports seem to relate to an identical craft', and he deduces that 'we are almost forced to an extraterrestrial, or other worlds, hypothesis'.[138] Tom Comella, on the other hand, asserts that 'the saucer evidence reveals more different types of objects and beings than the physical spaceship theory can logically account for',[36] while maverick commentator John Keel declares that we are left with two options: 'Either every object was individually constructed and utilized only once, or none of the objects really existed at all.'[88]

Twelve years have gone by since that last comment, and during that period we have learnt to accept that any attempt to explain the UFO in terms of current knowledge – whether that knowledge be of engineering or of any other scientific discipline – is liable to be inadequate.

Clearly, though, the UFO's diversity of appearance is one of its fundamental characteristics, and has to be one of the first elements to be covered by any hypothesis.

Similarly, we must not allow ourselves to be too impressed by the remarkable freedom from accident or breakdown the UFOs seem to enjoy. There have been many cases in which they seem to be grounded while their occupants busy themselves with apparent repairs, but there is, as Méheust has hinted,[101] something suspicious about the way in which they always get done in time; tomorrow morning's commuters, on their way to catch the 8.45, never pass the harassed ufonauts, with oily faces and grimy hands, still struggling to find the elusive fault.

There are many questions we would like to be able to answer about the UFOs themselves. Why is a certain type seen around for a while, then not again? Why do some have domes and windows suggesting occupants, while others seem hermetically sealed? Why do some have roaring furnace-blasts of flame, while others have no discernible 'power units'? Why are some bedecked with coloured and flashing lights while others are grey shapes slipping unobtrusively through our skies?

Surely there are good sound answers to these questions: but we may have to let go some of our human preconceptions before we are ready to accept them. And the same applies to their apparent defiance of what we are pleased to term 'laws of nature' – the physical parameters of movement that we on Earth have yet to find ways of exceeding. The UFOs are reported as moving at immense speeds – then stopping dead. They make abrupt ninety-degree changes of direction. They hover near the ground for long periods – then shoot off with instant acceleration. They manifest from seemingly nowhere and vanish as effectively. They change their physical shape and size, they seem able to divide and reunite in mid-air.

All these have been specifically reported, as we have seen in our review of the evidence; and they have been reported in connection with solid-seeming structured craft. If we accept the craft as fact, we must accept what is reported of their capability as fact also. And we need not be too reluctant to do so. Experts in the past told us that the human frame could not withstand speeds in excess of 50 km/h, that heavier-than-air flight was impossible, that the idea of flight to the moon was 'utter bilge'. Each in turn was proved mistaken: so it is likely to be with our present-day definers of boundaries. Clearly there are a lot of explanations due to us: but there is nothing in the nature of the objects themselves that is fundamentally incompatible with extraterrestrial origin.

* The behaviour of the UFOs is not so easy to reconcile with the extraterrestrial hypothesis, but then it is not easy to reconcile with *any* hypothesis. The objects seen high in the sky buzz about with the aimlessness of flies; those that approach the earth seem hardly more purposeful. Take just one example from many, the matter of lights. When one of our own aircraft displays lights, it does so for a purpose: to warn other aircraft of its position, or to identify itself, or to convey information, or to assist its own navigation. Sometimes the lights are associated with its propulsion – the flare of a jet engine, for example; or with its business – lighted cabin windows, say. But as we have seen, UFOs display lights in a quite different way, flashing them in sequence, alternating their colours, pulsing, blinking, rotating . . .

This is one of the many features of UFO behaviour that has prompted the more thoughtful ufologists to suspect that something more sophisticated is really behind it: that the UFOs are intentionally putting on some kind of display, perhaps as a teasing or inquiring puzzle, or alternatively that they do so in the same spirit as the set designer of a space fiction programme fills the cabin of the Starship 'Enterprise' with arrays of winking coloured lights as a quick way of saying, admire our sophisticated hardware! But what are the UFOs trying to say?

And why are some of them so keen to advertise their

presence while others keep the lowest profiles (not to speak of those that manage not to be observed at all, if any such exist)? Are some of them distracting our attention while others get on with more serious activities? But *what* activities? It is suggested that UFOs are seen in greater-than-average numbers in the vicinity of power installations, or research facilities, or missile bases: but even so, they are only a tiny percentage of the total: what are the rest of them here for? All that can be said of this curious lack of purpose is that though it may not help the extraterrestrial theory, neither does it support any other.

*The question of where the UFOs come from is one in which an anthropomorphic attitude has been allowed to prejudice the argument. Sceptics object that almost any interstellar journey would require many light years, often many lifetimes. Others reply that to think in terms of a literal real-time space journey is naive. The alleged visitors from UMMO, for example, claimed to make use of 'folds' in space which serve as short cuts;[128] and even if the UMMO communications turn out to be hoaxes, they indicate the sort of possibility we have no right to rule out.

Another objection is that the coincidence that the UFOs should visit us during the microscopic era of our Earth's history when it happens to be inhabited by a civilized species is too staggering to be believed. I agree: but may we not suppose an alien culture scanning the universe for signs of other civilizations, and also possessing the technical capability to visit us while we last?

A valuable source of information on this subject would be the UFO occupants themselves, and indeed one of the first bits of information to be transmitted, when an earthperson makes contact with an alien, is where he comes from. Unfortunately, it seems that every UFO hails from a different port. Sometimes they are from star systems known to us, the relatively close Alpha and Proxima Centauri being regular favourites: sometimes they are from unknown celestial bodies such as the planet

Clarion, home of Aura Rhanes, the space heroine of contactee Truman Bethurum's remarkable story.[16] She told him it was not surprising we Earthfolk did not know of Clarion's existence, for it is on the other side of the moon and hence invisible from here ... The UMMO case, incidentally, is the only one known to me which faces up to the very real difficulty of how exactly an alien visitor explains where he comes from, with no common names or reference numbers – and there are no compass points in space!

The extraterrestrial hypothesis can cope, up to a point, with most of the various complicating factors mentioned earlier in this chapter. The psychic connection can be accounted for by assuming the aliens to possess psychic powers, and writing off the rest of the phenomena as psychological side-effects of the sighting experience. The folklore connection can be explained easily in terms of our ancestors' efforts to account for extraterrestrial visitors – *too* easily, in fact, for this has led to a great many extravagant theories of the 'our ancestors came from outer space' variety.[109]

The BVM connection can be accommodated if we take the supposed Virgin to have been in reality a spaceperson, though it is not too easy to explain why such spacepersons should choose to appear to so demographically limited a section of the populace as underprivileged teenage girls in backward Catholic communities. The geophysical connection can be accounted for by explanations that range from the solidly material – the UFOs use an earth-grid to navigate by, or they suck up power from naturally-generated energy sources – to the occult, on which level it is liable to involve us with anything from geomancy to the Holy Grail, with dragons as the universal catalyst.[108, 77]

Where the extraterrestrial hypothesis falls severely short is in accounting for our Cases 7 to 10 – the foo fighters, ghost rockets and other UFOs of the past, along with a number of other fringe phenomena that seem to have only one thing in common, an assertive 'look-at-me!' quality which has encouraged some theorists to accuse the UFOs of 'putting on a show', for reasons we shall look at later.

I do not think any objective ufologist would deny that, of all the available hypotheses, that of extraterrestrial visitors best matches the evidence, despite a great many contradictions, implausibilities and inconsistencies. But there is one further objection, the most serious of all: it is that, after more than thirty years intensive study, during which the extraterrestrial hypothesis has dominated the field, there is not the slightest scrap of evidence that unequivocally supports it. We may accept that it covers more of the points more satisfactorily than any other proposed explanation; but it remains total conjecture.

UFOs as psychological manifestations

No open-minded UFO researcher has any doubt that a great many UFO reports are caused, or at any rate modified, by psychological and/or psychic processes related to the witness. The question is whether these processes are inherent in the phenomenon, either creating it or at any rate causing it to appear in the form in which it is perceived, or whether they are simply a by-product of the phenomenon, telling us nothing at all about the UFO but only about the alleged witness?

We can start by accepting, right away, that this latter process is undoubtedly true some of the time. There is no question that some witnesses are seeing natural phenomena or conventional artefacts, and perceiving them in all sincerity as alien spacecraft (see Cases 66 and 68). We can reasonably assume some kind of subconscious process that projects onto the innocent planet Venus the witness' personal preoccupations, hopes or fears.

Such a line of approach was put in a broader context by the Swiss psychologist C. G. Jung, whose book *Flying Saucers: A Modern Myth of Things in the Skies*,[83] though written so long ago as 1959, when we knew infinitely less about the phenomenon than we do today, shows astonishing insight into the relevance of the disc-shaped object from outer space for mankind at this crucial phase of its development. We can well accept that if a witness wants to project onto the external world a visionary something to symbolize his hopes and fears, then an alien spacecraft is appropriate; and the configuration of such a spacecraft may well be one that has archetypal resonance in our subconscious minds, as Jung claims disc-shapes have.

But do witnesses actually *create* the UFO they have this psychological need to see? Most champions of the psychological approach would shrink from such a claim. Generally they offer one of the following alternatives:

* The sight of something strange and inexplicable may, under certain circumstances – for example, if the witness is in a condition of anxiety, expectancy, depression or whatever – cause the witness to enter a dissociated state in which his subconscious mind is able to take over and substitute an illusion in place of reality. The scenario of that illusion will have been made-to-measure by his own subconscious (possibly by the same agency that fabricates his dreams) and so will be unique to him in some respects, while also drawing on various standard ingredients that he shares with his neighbours. Consequently, he will report an incident that is sufficiently like that of other witnesses to seem to fit into a recognized category of phenomena, yet is also sufficiently 'personalized' to encourage the belief that it was a real experience.[49, 124]

This is a recognized psychological process, which undoubtedly does occur in various contexts; so we need have no hesitation about supposing it capable of occurring in a UFO context. However, it clearly fails to account for cases where more than one person sees the same thing, forcing theorists to introduce the concept of collective hallucination, or telepathic hallucination, for which little if any evidence exists. Even more ingenuity is required to apply it to cases where there is instrumental or other non-human confirmation. In short, though this process may well prove to be the explanation for certain categories of case, it is manifestly inadequate to account for more than a small proportion.

*Alternatively, the illusion may be created by the object itself, or by those responsible for it. The UFO may be a hallucination created by some agency whose identity (the Devil? tricksy spirits? Cosmic Manipulators?) we can only speculate about. Or the UFO itself, inherently amorphous, may modify its appearance to conform to the expectation it discerns in the mind of the witness. This line of thinking has been carried to its furthest extreme by those who interpret the UFO in a mystical sense. For such speculators, its appearance is symbolic, its manifestation is a spiritual revelation, its purpose is to make us aware of another plane of reality.[154]

But if this is what UFOs are all about, we would expect to be able to discern some common factor in UFO sightings. It might be an attribute of the witness – some psychological trait they all share: or of the circumstances of the sighting – perhaps, that the witnesses were all in a favourable psychological state – tuned in, as it were, to the requisite wavelength to receive the signal. Perhaps such a common factor exists, but if so it is very elusive. UFO events seem to happen to all kinds of people in all kinds of states: for every witness who is half-asleep or in pensive mood, there is another who is caught by the UFO in the midst of life.

It is right that ideas such as these should be explored. If they did nothing else but awaken our minds to such possibilities, the UFOs will have done us a service. Unquestionably, a proportion of UFO sightings are no more than events in the psychological history of the witness. But to admit that UFOs have a psychological dimension is not to say that it is the only dimension they possess.

UFOs as cultural manifestations

What made it so difficult to believe the stories of Adamski and the other contactees was their claim that they had been individually 'chosen' by their alleged contacts; it is much easier to believe an abductee who seems simply to have been the guy who happened to be in the wrong place at the wrong time. Similarly, the fact that UFO experiences seem to occur to anyone, anywhere, makes it hard to see psychological theories as having more than a very limited application. Are there any hypotheses that retain the idea that UFOs are somehow not physically real, but do not require that therefore they must be individual hallucinations?

We have already come across some examples of UFOs interpreted as cultural manifestations: those that are attributed to Satan, or to the angelic forces opposing him. Once you have invoked supernatural forces of this kind, of course, you can invest them with whatever powers you choose: Satan can be supposed to build nuts-and-bolts UFOs as solid as an aeroplane – or to construct a simulacrum capable of fooling our perceptive senses.

Those who have outgrown devils and angels prefer to think in terms of cosmic forces, benevolent or otherwise: it is suggested that they make use of UFOs in the course of brainwashing us; but whether their aim is to deceive and distract us, or to raise our level of consciousness, depends on your point of view. French ufologist Jacques Vallée is the most coherent (not that that's saying very much) of such theorists: in a 1975 lecture[149] he suggested that the UFO phenomenon is the product of a very sophisticated technology. During the sighting, it is what it seems to be, a real, physical, material object. However, it is really only temporarily real: basically it is an illusion, taking on a transitory existence thanks to 'very advanced physical principles'. The purpose is cultural manipulation – possibly but not necessarily under the control of a form of non-human intelligence, and the physiological and psychological effects are a means to that end.

Four years later, Vallée added an extra dimension to his theory. While continuing to propose that the UFOs themselves are 'a manifestation of a reality that transcends our current understandings', he felt that some unknown force is exploiting them for its own ends. 'It is not the phenomenon itself, but the belief it has created, which is manipulated by human groups with their own objectives.'

That is to say, on the one hand we have the UFOs themselves, real though outside our present knowledge; and on the other, human beings exploiting this incomprehensibility in order to manipulate public opinion, and in so doing, creating a secondary phenomenon. We, in analyzing the evidence, must be careful to distinguish between, on the one hand, the 'true' UFOs, and on the other, the 'cultural' UFOs of the exploiters.

As regards the UFO itself, Vallée insists we are wrong to think in terms of 'spacecraft': 'The UFOs are physical manifestations that cannot be understood apart from their psychic and symbolic reality.'[154] Here he can reasonably be accused of hedging, but he deserves credit for sticking his neck out where most theorists are reluctant to commit themselves. By insisting that the UFO somehow combines physical and psychic attributes, Vallée is facing up to the phenomenon as he finds it, not distorting it to fit a preconceived explanation.

It is, admittedly, evasion of a sort to offer a hypothesis that presupposes purposes beyond our comprehension. But faced with a phenomenon that itself defies our comprehension, we cannot deny that he is being logical! And if Vallée's thinking is far out, it is far-out science, not a retreat into the occult.

In an earlier book on the subject, I concluded with this suggestion: 'Perhaps that is the secret of the UFO – a sum scribbled on a blackboard, seemingly meaningless to our eyes, but designed by some great teacher to stretch our minds a little further.'[50] As a hypothesis, the control-system scenario does not add up to much: but as a concept it adds a whole dimension to our thinking.

*   *   *   *

Natural phenomenon: terrestrial or extraterrestrial artefact: psychological or cultural manifestation? Each of these approaches deals more or less satisfactorily with some of the UFO evidence, while failing to account for the remainder. Are we asking for the unattainable, hoping for a single explanation that will accommodate each and every one of the cases we have studied in this inquiry? Could it be that we are looking at a *number* of phenomena, each with its own characteristics but also sharing others, so that each is liable to be confused with one or more of the others?

We see that some UFO theorists offer simple and plausible solutions – but at the cost of ignoring a part (sometimes a rather large part!) of the evidence: the geophysical hypothesis is an example of this. Others offer broad overall explanations, which fit well in some respects, not so well in others: the all-in-the-mind explanations typify this, but so also do the nuts-and-bolts extraterrestrial hypotheses. Yet others make bold suppositions which take minor obstacles in their stride, but for which no solid evidence exists, such as that the Devil or the United States Government are responsible. Even after thirty years the evidence for UFOs remains ambiguous: it tells us loud and clear that UFOs exist, but it answers with forked tongue when we ask what they are and where they come from.

EIGHT:
A PERSONAL ASSESSMENT

It would be a bold and reckless ufologist who would commit himself to anything but the most interim of guesses at the true nature of the UFO phenomenon. But evidence has been pouring in unabated for more than thirty years. If not we ourselves, then our friends and our neighbours are seeing these things and wondering what they are. It is surely incumbent on us to offer at least a provisional answer.

Here, then, and offered with the utmost diffidence, is my answer. First, I have not the slightest doubt that the UFO problem exists. The cases I have presented in these pages have intentionally been a mixed bag, designed to show how ambiguous – and often, how dubious – the phenomenon is, and also how often it can be explained in conventional terms. But I have already given, in Chapter Four, reasons for thinking that witnesses are, by and large, to be believed, and among the cases they report are many that I find utterly compelling, and what follows seems to me to be the minimum which that evidence requires.

I think it is clear, in the first place, that the UFO is not a single phenomenon. I think there are several things that we mistakenly lump together and give a collective label to, which is one reason they have for so long eluded us. I suggest there are no less than four sources of UFO reports:

1. I believe that a good many are *psychological* in origin. We know this is likely to be so in those instances where it

can be established that the witness did not have the experience he claims to have had, such as Case 68: I think it reasonable to surmise that similar processes are involved on many other occasions, for instance Cases 11, 13, 17 and 19.

This does not mean that such cases should be disregarded: on the contrary, they are of the greatest interest. For while the psychological processes may be known, the result of those processes, the specific form of the manifestation – the unique collage of the witness's individual preoccupations, his cultural background and the current space-age mythology of our times, woven together with the then-and-there circumstances of the particular time and place the incident occurs into a coherent and plausible fantasy so detailed and lifelike that the witness himself sincerely takes it for reality, and is often able to convince others as well – this is a phenomenon of the utmost significance, promising us a dramatic new insight into the human mind.

However, I would not for a moment suggest that this kind of explanation will account for more than a small proportion of the evidence. What it does is to remove some of the confusion from the evidence, by showing that some supposed UFO cases are actually 'pseudo-UFO cases', in which the witness – who is actually only a 'pseudo-witness' – uses the 'language' of the UFOs to express the story his subconscious needs to tell.

2. I believe that a proportion of UFOs are *natural biological objects*, which generally manifest as balls of light, but can possibly assume other shapes. What is more, I think these things possess intelligence: not very much, perhaps, but probably more than the majority of animals. I am willing to be persuaded that there is some link between these creatures and geophysical forces, but hitherto the evidence does not seem to me convincing: further research in this direction may establish such a connection or not. But some such explanation seems required by Cases 7 and 41,

to take just two examples, and also by Harley Rutledge's findings (Chapter One). Again, though, I do not see this explanation as accounting for more than a small percentage of the evidence.

3. I think there is a likelihood that some supposed UFOs are *devices being tested or operated* in secret by governments on earth. These may be man-made developments in the experimental stage or – though less probably, I feel – extraterrestrial craft operating with the connivance of Earth governments. I think this is the best explanation for cases such as 23 and 32, and perhaps for some others; but I think it inconceivable that such operations are being conducted on a scale capable of accounting for more than one case in a thousand. What such an explanation may do is remove from the dossier a number of particularly dramatic cases which at present are obscuring the overall picture.

4. I think there is a real probability, despite all the counter objections, that a great many UFOs are *structured artefacts of extraterrestrial origin*. I do not think we necessarily have an alien invasion on our hands, or face the prospect of imminent take-over: at worst it might be that some kind of surveillance operation is taking place, though even that seems to be being conducted in a remarkably sporadic and unworkmanlike manner. I am very conscious of the lack of supporting evidence, and also of the incongruousness of much of the evidence that we do have. I particularly feel the absence of any clear indication of purpose. But I see no other way to account for such cases as numbers 3, 5, 42, 44, 45, 54 and 65, all of which are multi-witness observations of objects that it does not seem possible were man-made.

BIBLIOGRAPHY AND READING LIST

This list is also a guide to further reading, especially for aspects that could not be adequately covered, such as John Michell's exploration of the Holy Grail connection.

** Essential reading.

* Recommended reading, generally in a specific area.

O Good all-round treatment of the subject.

! Thought-provoking, bizarre or simple old-fashioned fun.

It is important to read some of the bad books as well as the good, to get the subject in perspective. Only when you have read the first-person accounts of such alleged contactees as Angelucci and Bethurum can you form any conception of the serious nature of the contactee problem.

All books are published in Britain unless otherwise indicated.

Only a small proportion of these books and journals are obtainable from public libraries. The author will be glad to answer queries from serious researchers.

1   *ACUFOS Journal*, vol.3, no.6, Australian Centre for UFO Studies, Prospect S.A., Nov-Dec 1982.
2   ! Adamski, George, *Inside the Space Ships*, Spearman, 1956. Adamski – *see also* Leslie.
3   Adler, Bill, *Letters to the Air Force on UFOs*, Dell, New York, 1967.
4   ! Angelucci, Orfeo, *Secret of the Saucers*, Amherst Press, Wisconsin, 1955.
5   *APRO Bulletin*, July-August 1967 (Richardson case): May-June 1968 (Vidal case). Tucson, Arizona.

6   Arnold, Kenneth, and Palmer, Ray, *The Coming of the Saucers*, Amherst Press, Wisconsin, 1952.

7   Ballester Olmos, Vicente Juan, *OVNIs, El Fenomeno Aterrizaje*, Plaza and Janes, Barcelona, 1978.

8   Barry, James Dale, *Ball Lightning and Bead Lightning*, Plenum, New York, 1980.

9   Bastide, Jean, *La Memoire des OVNIs*, Mercure de France, Paris, 1978.

10   Beckley, Timothy Green, *The New World Order*, Global Communications, New York, 1982.

11   ! Bender, Albert, *Flying Saucers and the Three Men*, Saucerian Press, Clarksburg W. Vas., 1962.

12   Benitez, J J, *Ovnis, Documentos Officiales del Gobierno Espanol*, Plaza and Janes, Barcelona, 1977.

13   * Berlitz, Charles, and Moore, William L., *The Roswell Incident*, Grosset and Dunlap, NY, 1980.

14   Bernard, Raymond, *The Hollow Earth*, University Books, New Jersey, 1969.

15   Bessor, John, in *Fate*, March 1951, November 1967.

16   ! Bethurum, Truman, *Aboard a Flying Saucer*, De Vorss, Los Angeles, 1954.

17   Bloecher, Ted, *The UFO Wave of 1947*, private, 1967.

18   Blum, Ralph and Judy, *Beyond Earth*, Bantam, NY, 1974.

19   Boedec, Jean Francois, *Fantastiques Rencontres au bout du monde*, Le Signor, Quimper, 1982.

20   Boismont, A. Breire de, *On Hallucinations*, tr. Hulme, Renshaw, 1859.

21   Bondarchuk, Yurko, *UFO Sightings, Landings and Abductions*, Methuen, Toronto, 1980.

22   ** Bowen, Charles (ed.), *The Humanoids*, Spearman, 1969.

23   Bozzonetti, Yvan, *La Propulsion des Soucoupes Volantes*, privately by author and Ouranos group, 1975.

24   Brereton, Captain F. S., *The Great Aeroplane*, Blackie, 1911.

25   BUFORA, *Vehicle Interference Project*, 1979.

26   BUFORA Journal, vol.6, no.2, July-August 1977.

27   Butcher, Dan, *A Reference Book of UFO Sounds*, Surrey Investigation Group on Aerial Phenomena, 1969.

28   Campbell, Steuart, *Close Encounter at Livingston*, BUFORA 1982.

29   *Canadian UFO Report*, vol.1, no.7, 1968.

30 * Carrouges, Michel, *Les Apparitions de Martiens*, Fayard, Paris, 1963.

31 Cathie, Bruce L., *Harmonic 33*, 1968, *Harmonic 695*, 1971, *Harmonic 288*, 1977, Reed, Wellington N.Z.

32 Chambraud, Jean Pierre, *La Corse Base OVNI*, Du Rocher, Monaco, 1979.

33 * Clark, Jerome, and Coleman, Loren, *The Unidentified*, Warner, NY, 1975.

34 * Cohen, Daniel, *The Great Airship Mystery*, Dodd Mead, NY, 1981.

35 Cohn, Norman, *The Pursuit of the Millenium*, Secker and Warburg, 1957.

36 Comella, Tom (as Peter Kor), in *Flying Saucers*, Wisconsin, May 1966.

37 ** Condon, Edward U. (director), *Final Report of the Scientific Study of Unidentified Flying Objects*, University of Colorado, 1968.

38 Constable, Trevor James (as Trevor James), *They Live in the Sky*, New Age, Los Angeles, 1958, and *The Cosmic Pulse of Life*, Spearman, 1976.

39 Corliss, William, *Handbook of Unusual Phenomena*, Sourcebook Project, Maryland, 1977, quoting B. Maccabee in *Physics Today*, 1976.

40 Cramp, Leonard G., *Space, Gravity and the Flying Saucer*, Werner Laurie, 1954, and *Piece for a Jigsaw*, Somerton, 1966.

41 *CUFOS Bulletin*, Center for UFO Studies, Spring 1977.

42 CUFOS Conference Proceedings, 1976.

43 Delval, Pierre, *Contacts du 4e Type*, De Vecchi, Paris, 1979.

44 Devereux, Paul, *Earthlights*, Turnstone Press, 1982.

45 Eedle, Arthur, *The Christian Answer to the UFO Menace*, public address delivered at Warminster, 1979.

46 Evans, Hilary, 'Balls of Light' in *Probe Review*, vol.3, no.1, 1982.

47 Evans, Hilary, in *The Unexplained*, 1982-1983.

48 Evans, Hilary, in *Magonia*, no.8, 1982.

49 Evans, Hilary, 'Abducted by an Archetype', in *Fortean Times*, issue 33, 1980.

50 Evans, Hilary, *UFOs, The Greatest Mystery*, Albany Books, 1979.

51 *Exeter Express and Echo*, 23 August 1979.

52   Farish, Lucius, Newsclipping service, 1982.
53   *Fate*, April 1965.
54 * Festinger, Riecken, Schacter, *When Prophecy Fails*, Harper, NY, 1956.
55   Figuet, Michel, and Ruchon, Jean Louis, *OVNIs, Le Premier Dossier Complet*, Alain Lefeuvre, Nice, 1979.
56   *Flying Saucer Review*, vol.2, no.5 (Jansen); vol.11, nos.5 and 6 (Valensole); vol.20, no.2 (New Berlin); vol.22, no.4 (Himalayas); vol.24, no.4 (Partington); vol.25, no.1 (Sturno); vol.27, no.6 (Labrador); Special, *UFO Percipients* ('Dr X').
57   Fowler, Raymond, *UFOs, Interplanetary Visitors*, Exposition Press, NY, 1974.
58 * Fowler, Raymond, *The Andreasson Affair*, Prentice Hall, NY, 1979.
59 * Fuller, John G., *The Interrupted Journey*, Dial, NY, 1966.
60 * Fuller, John G., *Incident at Exeter*, Putnam, NY, 1966.
61   Fumoux, Jean Charles, *Preuves Scientifiques OVNI, l'Isocelie*, Du Rocher, Monaco, 1981.
62 O GABRIEL equipe, *Les Soucoupes Volantes, Le Grand Refus?* Moutet, Regusse, 1978.
63   Gardner, Edward L., in Conan Doyle, *The Coming of the Fairies*, Hodder and Stoughton, 1922.
64   Garreau, Charles, *Soucoupes Volantes, 25 Ans d'Enquêtes*, Mame, Paris, 1971.
65   GEPAN, *Notes Techniques no.6: A propos d'une Disparition,* Groupe d'Etudes des Phénomènes Aerospatiaux non Identifiés, Toulouse, 1981.
66   Grifol, Luis Jose, in *Hola!*, Madrid, April 1982 and elsewhere.
67 * Gross, Loren, *The Mystery of the Ghost Rockets*, private, California, 1974.
68 * Gross, Loren E., *Charles Fort, the Fortean Society, and Unidentified Flying Objects*, private, 1976.
69 * Gross, Loren, *UFOs, a History*, Arcturus, NY, 1982.
70   Guieu, Jimmy, *Blackout sur les Soucoupes Volantes*, Fleuve Noire, Paris, 1956.
71 ! Guieu, Jimmy, *Contacts OVNI Cergy-Pontoise*, Du Rocher, Monaco, 1980.
72   Haines, Richard F. (ed.), *UFO Phenomenon and the Behavioral Scientist*, Scarecrow Press, 1979.
73 ** Hall, Richard (ed.), *The UFO Evidence*, NICAP, Washington, 1964.

74   Harold, Clive, *The Uninvited*, Star books, 1979.
75   Helms, Harry, in *UFO Report*, NY, October 1977.
76 * Hendry, Allan, *The UFO Handbook*, Doubleday, NY, 1979.
77   Holiday, F. W., *The Dragon and the Disc*, Sidgwick and Jackson, 1973.
78 * Hynek, J. Allen, *The Hynek UFO Report*, Dell, NY, 1977.
79   *INFO Journal*, vol.1, no.3, Arlington, Va., 1968.
80   *Inforespace*, Brussels, no.4 (Namur photo); no.44 (Scornaux).
81   *International UFO Reporter*, vol.7, no.6, Centre for UFO studies.
82   Johnson, Frank, *The Janos People*, Spearman, 1980.
83 * Jung, Carl Gustav, *Flying Saucers, a Modern Myth*, Routledge and Kegan Paul, 1959.
84 * Keel, John A., *Operation Trojan Horse*, Putnam, NY, 1970.
85 * Keel, John A., *Strange Creatures from Time and Space*, Spearman, 1975.
86 * Keel, John A., *The Mothman Prophecies*, Dutton, NY, 1975.
87 * Keel, John A., *The Eighth Tower* (reprinted as *The Cosmic Question*), Dutton, NY, 1976.
88   Keel, John A., 'The Principle of Transmogrification', in *Flying Saucer Review*, July-August 1969.
89 ! King, George, *The Day the Gods Came*, Aetherius Society, Los Angeles, 1965.
90 ! Klarer, Elizabeth, *Beyond the Light Barrier*, Timmins, Cape Town, 1980 (first published in German, 1977).
91 ! Klass, Philip J., *UFOs identified*, Random House, NY, 1968.
92 * Klass, Philip J., *UFOs Explained*, Random House, NY, 1974.
93   Knight, David C., *UFOs, a Pictorial History*, McGraw Hill, NY, 1979.
94 * Lawson, Alvin H., 'The Abduction Experience, a Testable Hypothesis', in *Magonia*, no.10, 1982.
95 ! Leslie, Desmond, with Adamski, George, *Flying Saucers Have Landed*, Werner Laurie, 1953.
96   Lind, Tom, *The Catalogue of UFO Periodicals*, Said of saucers, Florida, 1982.
97   *Lumières dans la Nuit*, Chambon-sur-Lignon, France, no.194 (Lagarde); no.191 (Seignes); no.197 St Mandrier); no.202 (Menton); no.206 (Laborie case and Cornu article); no.207 (Trans-en-Provence); Contact-Lecteurs Mars 1972 (Dax).

98 * McCampbell, James M., *Ufology*, Jaymac, Belmont, Ca., 1973.

99 Maclellan, Alec, *The Lost World of Agharti*, Souvenir, 1982.

100 ! Mattern, W., *UFOs – Unbekanntes Flugobjekt?* Samisdat, Toronto, early 1960s.

101 * Méheust, Bertrand, *Science Fiction et Soucoupes Volantes*, Mercure de France, Paris, 1978.

102 ! Menger, Howard, *From Outer Space to You*, Saucerian, W. Va., 1959.

103 ! Menzel, Donald H., *Flying Saucers*, Harvard University Press, Mass., 1953.

104 ! Menzel, Donald H., with Boyd, Lyle G., *The World of Flying Saucers*, Doubleday, NY, 1963.

105 ! Menzel, Donald H., with Taves, Ernest H., *The UFO enigma*, Doubleday, NY, 1977.

106 O Michel, Aimé, *Lueurs sur les Soucoupes Volantes*, Mame, Paris, 1954 (*The Truth about Flying Saucers*, Hale, 1957).

107 * Michel, Aimé, *Mysterieux Objets Celestes*, Paris, 1957 (?), (*Flying Saucers and the Straight-line Mystery*, Criterion, NY, 1958).

108 Michell, John, *The Flying Saucer Vision*, Sidgwick and Jackson, 1967.

109 Misraki, Paul (as Paul Thomas), *Les Extraterrestres*, Plon, Paris, 1962 (*Flying Saucers through the Ages*, Spearman, 1965).

110 * Monnerie, Michel, *Et si les OVNIs n'existaient pas?*, Les Humanoides Associés, Paris, 1977.

111 * Monnerie, Michel, *Le Naufrage des Extra-terrestres*, Nouvelles éditions rationalistes, Paris, 1979.

112 Moravec, Mark, in *Journal of Australian Centre for UFO Studies*, vol.1, no.3, Prospect, S.A., June 1980.

113 * NICAP, *Electro-magnetic Effects Associated with UFOs,* Washington, 1960.

114 * NICAP, *UFOs, a New Look*, Washington, 1969.

115 Oberg, James, in *Saga's UFO Report*, NY, August 1980.

116 Olsen, Thomas J., *The Reference for Outstanding UFO Reports*, Maryland, 1966.

117 ! Paget, Peter, *The Welsh Triangle*, Panther, 1979.

118 Pawlicki, T. B., *How to Build a Flying Saucer*, Prentice Hall, New Jersey, 1981.

119   *Phénomènes Spatiaux*, Paris, no.26 (Pontejos); no.45 (very small UFOs).
120   Pinotti, Roberto, *UFO, la Congiura di Silenzio*, Armenia, Milano, 1974.
121   Prachan, Jean, *Le Triangle des Bermudes, Base Secrète des OVNIs*, Belfond, Paris, 1978.
122   *Probe Report*, Bristol, vol.2, nos.3 and 4, 1982.
123   Pugh, Randall Jones, and Holiday, F. W., *The Dyfed Enigma*, Faber, 1979.
124 * Randles, Jenny, and Warrington, Peter, *UFOs, a British Viewpoint*, Hale, 1979.
125   *Rapportnytt*, Bergen, vol.1, 1981.
126   *Revue des Soucoupes Volantes*, Regusse, France, 1978.
127   Ribera, Antonio, *Treinta Anos de Ovnis*, Plaza and Janes, Barcelona, 1982.
128   Ribera, Antonio, *El Misterio de Ummo*, Plaza and Janes, Barcelona, 1979.
129   Rimmer, John, *Alien Abductions*, Aquarian Press, 1984.
130   *Rocky Mountain Conference Proceedings*, co-ordinator Leo Sprinkle, Laramie, Wyoming, 1980.
131 ** Rutledge, Harley D., *Project Identification*, Prentice Hall, NY, 1981.
132 ** Sagan, Carl, and Page, Thornton, *UFOs, a Scientific Debate*, Cornell University Press, NY, 1972.
133   Salisbury, Frank, in *Proceedings of the First International UFO Congress*, Warner, NY, 1980.
134 * Sanderson, Ivan T., *Uninvited Visitors*, Cowles, NY, 1967.
135 * Sanderson, Ivan T., *Invisible Residents*, Crowell, NY, 1970.
136   Smith, Frederick W., *Cattle Mutilation, the Unthinkable Truth*, Freedland, Colorado, 1976.
137   *Stendek*, Madrid, no.9, August 1972.
138   Stevens, Wendelle C., 'Seeing is Believing' in *Saga's UFO Report*, Fall 1974.
139   Stevens, Wendelle C., with Herrmann, Bill, *UFO Contact from Reticulum*, private, Arizona, 1981.
140 ** Story, Ronald D., *The UFO Encyclopedia*, New English Library, 1980.
141 O Story, Ronald D., *UFOs and the Limits of Science*, New English Library, 1981.
142 ! Stranges, Frank E., *(Stranger at the Pentagon*, IEC Book Division, 1967.

143 *   Stringfield, Leonard H., 'Retrievals of the Third Kind', in *UFO OHIO Yearbook*, 1979; *The UFO Crash/ Retrieval Syndrome, Status Report II*, MUFON, 1980; *UFO Crash/Retrievals, Status Report III*, private, Ohio, 1982.

144   *Texarkana Gazette*, 28 October 1981.

145   Trench, Brinsley le Poer, *Secret of the Ages: UFOs from inside the Earth*, Souvenir, 1974.

146   *UFO, Tidskrift for UFO-Norge*, January 1982.

147   *Ufologia*, supplement to Clypeus, issue no.6, Torino.

148   *The Unexplained*, vol.9, p.2121 (Cash-Landrum case), Orbis, 1982.

149   Vallée, Jacques, in *Thesis-Antithesis*, Proceedings of 1975 symposium of AIAA and World Futures Society.

150 *   Vallée, Jacques, *Anatomy of a Phenomenon*, Regnery, Chicago, 1965.

151 *   Vallée, Jacques, with Janine Vallée, *Challenge to Science*, Regnery, Chicago, 1966.

152 *   Vallée, Jacques, *Passport to Magonia*, Regnery, Chicago, 1965.

153 *   Vallée, Jacques, *The Invisible College*, Dutton, NY, 1975.

154 *   Vallée, Jacques, *Messengers of Deception*, And/Or Press, California, 1979.

155 *   Vesco, Renato, *Intercettateli Sensa Sparare*, Mursia, Milano, 1968 (*Intercept but Don't Shoot*, Grove Press, NY, 1971); *I velivoli del misterio*, Mursia, 1969;   *Operazione pleni- luni*, Mursia, 1972.

156 !   Vorilhon, Claude ('Rael'), *Le Livre qui dit la Verité*, Editions du message, France, 1974.

157   Warren, Donald I., 'Status Inconsistency Theory and Flying Saucer Sightings', in *Science*, November 1970.

158   Wells, Alice K., in *Gray Barker's Book of Adamski*, Saucerian, circa 1965.

159 !   Wilson, Clifford, and Weldon, John, *Close Encounters, a Better Explanation*, Master Books, California, 1978.

160   Winder, R. H. B., *Design for a Flying Saucer*, reprint from *Flying Saucer Review*, 1966-1967.

161 *   Zurcher, Eric, *Les Apparitions d'Humanoides*, Lefeuvre, Nice, 1979.

INDEX